He's Making Diamonds

He's Making Diamonds:

A Teen's Thoughts on Faith Through Chronic Illness

S.G. Willoughby

Printed in the United States of America
First Printing, 2018
ISBN: 978-1722668792
sgwilloughby.com

This book is not intended as a substitute for the medical advice of physicians. The reader should regularly consult a physician in matters relating to his/her health and particularly with respect to any symptoms that may require diagnosis or medical attention.

Cover design by Dan Sirak, Jolt Studios.
Interior design & formatting by Kellyn Roth, kellynroth.blog.
Editing by Kelsey Bryant.
Foreword by Jon Steingard.
Author photograph by J. Silas Willoughby.
Scriptures taken from the Holy Bible, New International Version®, NIV®. Copyright © 1973, 1978, 1984, 2011 by Biblica, Inc.™ Used by permission of Zondervan. All rights reserved worldwide. www.zondervan.com The "NIV" and "New International Version" are trademarks registered in the United States Patent and Trademark Office by Biblica, Inc.™

Dedication

To all my support system; you're amazing!

But especially to Daddy, Mama, Silas, and Nina. I don't have the words. This book would not exist without you, and you have been there for me through so much.

Most of all, I write this for my King. This book is completely and entirely His.

Contents

Foreword
Introduction
1. Where and Why
2. Something Changed
3. The Pit of Despair and the Fight for Joy
4. Communication in Chronic Illness
5. Relationships in Chronic Illness
6. Teenager, Child, or Adult?
7. Hope and Disappointments
8. Resting in the Storm
9. Peace in Storms
10. Just Keep Praying
11. Moving Mountains
12. In My Weakness
13. He's Making Diamonds

Foreword

It's not fair.

Life—it just isn't fair.

You're not imagining it. It's not all in your head. It's not you "being dramatic." There are things in your life that have brought you pain—things that so many other people don't seem to have to deal with. Sometimes you might look around and wonder what life would be like if you had it as easy as "they do."

I want you to know it's okay to admit that it hurts. That it sucks. That it feels unfair.

Life is mysterious. I have no idea why certain struggles and burdens rest on the shoulders of the people they do. It can be confusing to understand the idea of a loving God when we're faced with a horrible illness, abuse, or other deeply difficult situation. I can honestly say I don't understand how it all works.

However—I have seen some things that make it impossible to believe that there is such a thing as hopeless.

A few years back, I was a part of writing a song called "Diamonds." In the previous several years I had seen God do amazing things in some of my friends and family's lives, using their hardest moments as a vehicle to bring good, wonderful things into their lives.

For instance, my sister went through treatment for cancer while she was in her early twenties, and I watched God bring our family into a new season of closeness because of that process. She is alive and well today, and I wonder if we would be as close now if it wasn't for that horrible treatment we all walked my sister through together. I think we all gained a new appreciation for each other during that season.

I spent a lot of time thinking about how God redeems our struggles and even uses them to bring joy into our lives later on. I thought the formation of a diamond was a beautiful metaphor for this idea.

If you're not familiar, diamonds are formed when ordinary coal and rocks are squeeeeeeeezed really hard and heated up really hot, enduring this pressure underground for long pieces of time. It's the only way to make a diamond.

No heat? No pressure? No diamond!

That heat and pressure takes something ordinary and makes it extraordinary. It takes something dirty and makes it shine. It takes something soft and makes it the strongest substance on earth.

In the same way, I believe God uses our hardest times and most difficult circumstances to shape and mold us into stronger, more beautiful, more extraordinary people.

Some of the kindest, strongest, most incredible people I've ever met have been through incredible hardship. I can't see that as a coincidence.

Sara is one of those people to me. The health challenges she has could have caused her to become bitter toward God and people, and wall herself off from others. Instead she was inspired to write this book in the hopes that her story can encourage you.

I find that incredible.

Sara is the first to say she doesn't have all the answers. The questions that have led you to read this book, the same questions that Sara has asked herself, aren't always easily answered. However, she has taken a step back from her circumstances and has found a perspective on them that I am certain has brought her so much peace, and even joy, even in the middle of her pain.

It's my hope for you that this book will help you take a step back as well, and see how God might end up using these struggles of yours in a positive way in your life, and the lives of those around you.

No matter what things look like right now, I really do believe He's making a diamond in you right now.

Jon Steingard

Frontman for Hawk Nelson

July 2018

Introduction

Dear Teenager with a Long-Term Illness,

I want you to know that I've been praying for you all throughout the long days of typing, editing, and rewriting. This book is for you. I used to think that I was the only one. That I was all alone as someone who was young and sick.

I mean, looking around, it sure seemed that way! Everyone else seemed to take health for granted—just as I once had. As I spent more and more days in bed, everyone else was hanging out with friends. When I worried about what in the world was wrong with my failing body, the other teenagers around me were concerned about school. Ring a bell?

But I'm here to tell you that you are not alone. Not by a long shot.

You see, as I began to search for people like me, someone who could understand, I was at a loss to find blogs, websites, books— anything! Now I know that I should have just kept looking, but not knowing that I decided to start my own blog and titled it "R535," just to see what would happen. I had learned some things from my illness and wanted to share. I wanted to tell my story and help people understand.

Turns out, I wasn't alone. And neither are you. Soon, I began to connect with others who, like me, lived with a chronic illness (or two or three). "What? Me too!"

Me too.

And from those "me toos" this book was born.

I have Lyme disease, toxic black mold poisoning, and multiple chemical sensitivity. It all started on July 23, 2015. We didn't know it yet, but we were living in a house contaminated by eleven different toxic molds.

In my family, I turned out to be the canary in the coal mine. The sick one in the toxic mold house. Although most of the family eventually developed various forms of symptoms related to the mold we were all exposed to, for some reason I was the one who reacted the worst, ending up bedridden. My symptoms include, but are not limited to, brain fog, joint pain, muscle weakness and failure, eye problems, sensory issues, anxiety, depression, various digestive problems, liver, gallbladder, and other organ issues, dizziness, nausea, and more.

Sound familiar?

Through clearly God-orchestrated events, we found a safe, clean house. But while that helped for a time, eventually I grew worse again. New symptoms appeared—ones I didn't know how to deal with.

Eventually, it got so bad that I found myself in bed, unable to physically hold myself up, too weak to move or take care of myself. Finally, we found a doctor who was able to help. She was the seventh one we tried.

Sickness affects all parts of your life, and faith isn't exempt. I don't have all the answers. But what I do have is a lot of questions. How do we reconcile the two? Why does God let us suffer? Have we lost our childhood? How does this affect our future? And what about relationships with people? How do you hold on to hope when it's continually disappointed?

All those questions you haven't yet dared to verbalize or admit? They're okay. And they have answers. Someone else also has the same questions, somewhere. And in this book, I'm going to address some of the ones I've asked. The ones I've brought to God, and that He has allowed me to learn from.

Like I said, I don't have all the answers. But I do have a lot of questions. To be completely honest with you, I don't feel qualified to write this book. I'm young. I'm no theologian. I'm just a sick teenage girl. And I know that so many of you reading this have suffered so much more than I have. Many of you have suffered for ten years or more, and I'm only in the two- to three-year mark.

But God's grace is sufficient. I pray that God may use this book to encourage you as you try to walk with faith through illness and trials, whatever they may be.

Therefore, without further ado, turn the page, and let us begin this adventure!

Your sister in Christ,

Sara

1. Where and Why

"I love You so much. Thank You for the answers."
-Sara's journal, March 4, 2017

Where is God in the midst of suffering?

"God? Where are You?" Where did He go? He was just here . . . But how could God be with us in the middle of the suffering we are going through? How could He allow it? Something about 'Good Father' and the pain we see all around us just doesn't seem to match up! Has God abandoned us to wander around in this misery, giving us up as a lost cause? *Are* we a lost cause? Or . . . Is God intentionally putting us through this hurt, this pain, this struggle?

How can God and pain coexist in our lives? Do we dare even ask these questions? I can't help it! My heart has to know. Doesn't yours?

Here's the good news: God can stand up to any question you or I ask of Him. He is so much bigger than our doubts or questions. He will never be defeated by them. There is no question we can ask that will make Him any less.

Cast all your anxiety on him because he cares for you. (1 Peter 5:7)

David, the man after God's own heart, asks in Psalm 22:1, "My God, my God, why have you forsaken me? Why are you so far from saving me, so far from my cries of anguish?" Even Jesus Himself repeats these words of David's as He hangs on the cross in Matthew 27:46 and Mark 15:34.

It is not wrong to ask questions. Actually, much of this book came from questions that I've wrestled with and brought to God. The devil wants us to think that we can't talk to God (or anyone) about our questions. He doesn't want us to face them head-on. He doesn't want us to bring them into the light. The devil wants us to be trapped in guilt. He wants us to be separated from God. He wants these questions to put up a barrier between us and God (or even other Christians). The way to overcome this is to simply ask the questions! Not to try to forget them, bury them, or hide them.

Where Is God in Suffering?

Therefore, let me ask again: Where is God in the midst of suffering?

Almost a year ago, I wrote the following in my journal, along with a long list of Scriptures:

"When You seem farthest, that is when You are closest."

Think of Job. When we read the book of Job in the Bible, we can see God is very involved in Job's trials from the beginning. The thing is, Job can't see that. He doesn't know what's happening in the first three chapters of the book. He doesn't know what's at stake. Job doesn't see God meeting with Satan, pointing Job, himself, out. God never once speaks to Job or shows His presence to this servant of His until the very end of the book.

God is silent even when Job loses everything: sons and daughters, material goods, servants, and health. Even as Job sits in misery and pain, being told off by his friends (who think they are *helping* him).

But God was certainly there! God was silent, but He hadn't left. He wasn't busy with other matters. After all, God is omnipresent. God wasn't turning a blind eye as Job, the "righteous man," suffered. Quite the opposite! God had staked His reputation on this human man. All of Heaven was watching Job's every move to see how he would respond.

In my alarm I said, "I am cut off from your sight! Yet you heard my cry for mercy when I called to you for help". (Psalm 31:22)

Another example is Joseph, the son of Jacob. He went through a whole lot of ups and downs in his life . . . from son, to slave, to favored, to prisoner. Where was God in that? Where was God when Joseph was sold by his own family? Where was God when Joseph was falsely accused? Why would He have let this righteous man suffer so? As we know from the Bible, God was right there, orchestrating the whole thing.

Where was God when these righteous people cried out from the painful depths of their heart to the God who seemed to have forsaken them? He was right there. And He is right here with us too. When God seems the farthest from us, He is really the closest. He cares so much for us. He will never forsake us or abandon us. Just look at these two verses:

God has said, "Never will I leave you; never will I forsake you." *(Hebrews 13:5b)*

And also,

Those who know your name trust in you, for you, Lord, have never forsaken those who seek you. (Psalm 9:10)

As readers of Job's and Joseph's stories, we can easily see that God was right there with them, orchestrating everything. But they couldn't see that part. All they could see was the trial in front of them. I experienced the same thing. One time, I was feeling especially far away from God. It felt like no matter what I did, I was separated from Him. Logically, I knew that He was there, but I couldn't feel His presence. To me, it felt like I was far away from God. But in reality, He was working in my heart and life and in the lives of those around me during that time. He was there, even if I didn't feel like it.

Has God abandoned you? Believe me, I know it can feel like it sometimes, but all we have to do is open our eyes to see that He is right here with us. He will never leave us to fight alone. He is with us even in the darkest times. Even trapped in a well, or a dungeon, or as a slave, He is working everything for our good.

The righteous cry out, and the Lord hears them; he delivers them from all their troubles. The Lord is close to the brokenhearted and saves those who are crushed in spirit. The righteous person may have many troubles, but the Lord delivers him from them all; he protects all his bones, not one of them will be broken.
(Psalm 34:17–20)

Promised Troubles

Which brings us to the next question: why? We've established that God is with us in our trials even if sometimes we don't feel like it. But . . . why in the world would He allow them to happen to us in the first place? How can a good God allow His children to suffer? If He is in control of everything, how could He allow this to happen? Especially to "good" people? Especially to Christians?

Why would God, if He loves us, allow us to go through such pain and suffering? Can you believe that He has a purpose in it? A plan? No, if I say that, it just makes it seem worse, doesn't it? God planned this for you? For me? How could He do that to us, His children?

Often people think that once they are saved, life should be perfect. Life should be good. We should be blessed. We should have an invisible shield around us and those we love. While it is true that God is protector and that He wants to bless us if we obey Him (and it's important we don't forget or lose sight of that!), the fact is that we live in a fallen world. A fallen, sinful, hurting, and broken world.

In the Garden of Eden, everything was absolutely perfect. Because no taint of sin was yet in the world, there were none of the consequences of sin either. There was no suffering, no pain, no sickness, no death—not even briers and thorns! But when sin came into the world through humanity's own choice, all that changed. While God loves us beyond anything we can imagine, and while He is a merciful God, our God is also a just God. He cannot just sweep away the punishment that was brought on the earth for humanity's sin.

4

God doesn't promise us a joyride through life. No, He actually promises us trials and assures us that there will be struggles. Right before Jesus was crucified, He told this to His disciples in John 16:33:

"I have told you these things, so that in me you may have peace. In this world you will have trouble. But take heart! I have overcome the world."

God doesn't apologize for the troubles. It's not His fault, after all! He won't apologize for the trials you or I are in right now. As Katie Davis says in her book *Kisses from Katie*:

"This is Jesus. Not that He apologizes for the hard and the hurt, but that He enters in, He comes with us to the hard places."

However, while the consequences of sin are unavoidable, God has overcome the world through Jesus' sacrifice, and we can be free from sin, which is the root of the problem.

Again, let's go back to the heroes of the Bible, the champions of faith. David, the man after God's own heart, spent years living in caves, hunted unjustly by his own father-in-law, King Saul. Job, the righteous man on whom God staked His reputation, lost *everything*. Moses, God's chosen servant to free His people, spent forty years in hiding from Pharaoh, living as a shepherd in the desert, only to lead the people of Israel through *another* forty years in the desert, to the border of the promised land, which he didn't even get to set foot in!

Many of God's prophets spent their lives in very unpleasant ways, in the midst of war and sin and persecution. The apostles, spreading God's good news in obedience to Him, often faced torture. Eleven out of the twelve died by execution, after living lives on the move. Jesus—though God's Son, though perfect—suffered a most gruesome death.

In Psalm 73, the psalmist asks the same question: Why do "good" people suffer? He didn't understand why he had bothered to strive for righteousness and godliness when all he got for it was pain;

meanwhile, the wicked people around him were thriving and prosperous. It just didn't seem fair! But look at verses 13–20:

Surely in vain I have kept my heart pure and have washed my hands in innocence. All day long I have been afflicted, and every morning brings new punishments. If I had spoken out like that, I would have betrayed your children. When I tried to understand all this, it troubled me deeply till I entered the sanctuary of God; then I understood their final destiny. Surely you place them on slippery ground; you cast them down to ruin. How suddenly are they destroyed, completely swept away by terrors! They are like a dream when one awakes; when you arise, Lord, you will despise them as fantasies.

God showed the psalmist their end. We will talk about this much more in a coming chapter, but our time on earth is such a short time in the span of eternity. The wicked will spend that eternity in Hell. But those of us who have chosen to accept God's salvation will spend eternity in Heaven!

Do We Deserve to Be Healthy?

If we are "good" people or Christians, though, don't we *deserve* to be healthy? Is it our "right" to be healthy?

The answer is an unpleasant no. Humans are flawed and sinful. None of us can do anything at all to deserve God's mercy and grace. We don't *deserve* to be healthy. In fact, we deserve just the opposite, as we talked about earlier.

For it is by grace you have been saved, through faith—and this is not from yourselves, it is the gift of God—not by works, so that no one can boast. (Ephesians 2:8–9)

Paul was the one who wrote that. If anyone could earn God's grace, it was him. He was not just a normal Jew; he was a Pharisee. He himself declares:

"For it is we who are the circumcision, we who serve God by his Spirit, who boast in Christ Jesus, and who put no confidence in the flesh—though I myself have reasons for such confidence. If someone else thinks they have reasons to put confidence in the flesh, I have more: circumcised on the eighth day, of the people of Israel, of the tribe of Benjamin, a Hebrew of Hebrews; in regard to the law, a Pharisee; as for zeal, persecuting the church; as for righteousness based on the law, faultless." (Philippians 3:3–6)

That's not all of it, though! Once he became a Christian, he was one of the apostles. He even wrote much of the New Testament! No one doubts his faith. And yet...

And yet, he was given a thorn in his side (see 2 Corinthians 12:7). He was allowed to suffer immensely, as he describes in 2 Corinthians 11:21–30:

To my shame I admit that we were too weak for that! Whatever anyone else dares to boast about—I am speaking as a fool—I also dare to boast about. Are they Hebrews? So am I. Are they Israelites? So am I. Are they Abraham's descendants? So am I. Are they servants of Christ? (I am out of my mind to talk like this.) I am more. I have worked much harder, been in prison more frequently, been flogged more severely, and been exposed to death again and again. Five times I received from the Jews the forty lashes minus one. Three times I was beaten with rods, once I was pelted with stones, three times I was shipwrecked, I spent a night and a day in the open sea, I have been constantly on the move. I have been in danger from rivers, in danger from bandits, in danger from my fellow Jews, in danger from Gentiles; in danger in the city, in danger in the country, in danger at sea; and in danger from false believers. I have labored and toiled and have often gone without sleep; I have known hunger and thirst and have often gone without food; I have been cold and naked. Besides everything else, I face daily the pressure of my concern for all the churches. Who is weak, and I do not feel weak? Who is led into sin, and I do not inwardly burn? If I must boast, I will boast of the things that show my weakness.

So, do we deserve health? Do we deserve a perfect life because we are "good people" and Christians? Nope.

But . . . Why?

"Okay," you say. "I get it. God did not promise us a life of ease. He promised us trouble. But *why*? If He loves us, *why* in the world would He allow us to go through this?"

Well, believe it or not, I finally came to this conclusion and realization sometime in the middle of months in bed, in pain, without answers: *"This, too, is an expression of Your love, God."* Those were the words I wrote into my journal.

This trial, anything and everything you are facing, is an expression of God's love for you and for me. I know. How can that be? It doesn't make much logical sense. At least, not at first glance. But God gives us these things as gifts. He gives us what He knows we are strong enough, in Him, to handle. He gives us only what will grow us, grow our faith, and prepare us for the plans He has for us in the future!

He truly has a plan in this.

Let me say it again: God has a plan. More than that, it's a *good* plan.

For he does not willingly bring affliction or grief to anyone. (Lamentations 3:33)

Something that comes to mind as I think through this topic is a quote I came across a while ago:

"God is more interested in your character than your comfort." -Rick Warren

As hard as it can be for us to grasp, God allows us to have the trials we do because He loves us. We can't see everything, but He can. He sees it all. He sees that this is something we need for our faith, for our growth, and more. His ways are perfect. I know this may sound cliché, and hard to hear at the same time. I know it seems like the simple Sunday school answer, but guys, it's true! James 1:2–4 says,

Consider it pure joy, my brothers and sisters, whenever you face trials of many kinds, because you know that the testing of your faith produces perseverance. Let perseverance finish its work so that you may be mature and complete, not lacking anything.

In those forty years spent as a shepherd, Moses learned the skills he would need to lead an entire nation through the wilderness. While living in caves, David learned to lead a people full of zeal, ideas, and disagreements. While a mere shepherd boy, he learned to be a warrior, to be a humble man after God's heart . . . skills David would need later to be king of Israel.

God loves us.

This has been the hardest season of my life, by far. But it has been the one in which I have grown the most in my faith, my maturity, and who I am.

Let me offer you some hope, though: *this will end.* There is a light at the end of the tunnel. There is an end. I know it seems impossible. I know it seems so far away. I know. But it is true. I promise, it is true. God promises that when we are in Him, there is relief, whether it is here or in Heaven. We will live in complete health and freedom in Heaven. This will end. Hold on to that, as I have!

Job, when in the midst of pain, grief, and sorrow, begged that God would turn His eye from him, that Job could live the short time he had and then die. But God eventually restored all that he had lost: his health, his wealth, and everything that had been torn so brutally from him. Ultimately though, Job got to spend eternity in Heaven with the King. Just like Job, God still loves you. He has a plan in this. He is with you. There is an end to the suffering.

And he who searches our hearts knows the mind of the Spirit, because the Spirit intercedes for God's people in accordance with the will of God. And we know that in all things God works for the

good of those who love him, who have been called according to his purpose. For those God foreknew he also predestined to be conformed to the image of his Son, that he might be the firstborn among many brothers and sisters. (Romans 8:27–29)

We may not understand God's plan. But that doesn't mean He doesn't have one and that it isn't good.

Think of David. God's plan was to make him king of Israel. God even told David this when he was a young boy. What God didn't tell David was that it would be fifteen years of trials before that was to happen. But those trials were exactly what David needed to equip him to be king.

He chose David his servant and took him from the sheep pens; from tending the sheep he brought him to be the shepherd of his people Jacob, of Israel his inheritance. And David shepherded them with integrity of heart; with skillful hands he led them. (Psalm 78:70–72)

It's the same with us. God has a perfect plan; we just have to trust Him. He may be giving us our individual trials to prepare and equip us for our future gifts.

Take It Deeper

- At the end of each chapter, there will be a brief section with a suggested action that you can take to understand the topic at a deeper level. To not just read it, but to make it your own and take action. I realize that this can be hard to do sometimes when your brain or body isn't functioning very well due to sickness, so right now I'm going to give you permission to skip these sections if you're getting hung up on them. It's okay. You can always come back to them. I want this book to be encouraging . . . not burdensome. However, if you feel up to it, please take the time to search out the topics we're discussing on your own and take action to grow in your faith. Don't just take my word for things. Pray and ask God to open your eyes to see His truth.

- For this first chapter, here's your assignment: Write down all of your "why" questions, all of the questions you haven't yet dared to voice. Ask God where He is and why He's doing this. Ask things like "Why me?" and "Why now?" and "Why would You allow this?" and "How can a loving God let His children suffer?" Don't hold back. It doesn't have to be only big questions, either. I have made this same list before. Mine included things from asking what the purpose of my sickness was, to asking why I couldn't eat something as simple as eggs because of food sensitivities.

S.G. Willoughby

2. Something Changed

"God's love is far deeper than any pain."
-Sara's journal, January 10, 2017

Practical Life Changes

The first Christmas after getting sick, I had severe joint pain—so much so that I could not wrap or unwrap any presents. Of course, that was not the only practical way my life had to change to accommodate my illness. I couldn't eat any of the holiday foods, for one. I had never noticed before how many of our holidays are centered around food! It didn't bother me too much at the time, though I do remember shedding some tears over it. It had been five months since I got sick, and I had hoped to be better five months earlier.

When my birthday came six months later, however, that was rather more difficult both mentally and emotionally. We had moved away from friends, I was feeling pretty horrible (*still*), I couldn't have birthday cake, and life was incredibly hard. Some of these things are petty, I know, but sometimes the smallest things are the hardest things.

However, those are by no means the only ways my life has been affected practically by my sickness. No, things like brain fog, chemical sensitivity, and other nasty symptoms make my life *much* different from many of the people around me. It's extremely difficult to go out in public. It's a constant battle to find clothes that don't burn my skin from chemicals. It's so hard not being able to think clearly and keep up a normal conversation, do normal day-to-day tasks, or even do school for that matter.

Before, I loved to go on long runs or hikes. Then, I sat on my bottom to go down the stairs in our home. Now we don't have stairs, since we had to up and move because of the mold.

Things have changed in my life. But even more than these practical limitations, *I* have changed in much deeper ways.

"Impactful."

"Refinement."

"Stronger."

"Humbling."

I asked some people who had a chronic illness what one word they would use to describe long-term sickness. Those are some of the words they chose. (There is also one other word used even more than those, but more on that one in chapter eight.) What do all of those words have in common? Change. More specifically, people changing.

I Lost Me

I followed my mom around the grocery store, a white-blond head bobbing along in her wake. Soon, my young self got caught up in examining all of the colorful boxes and foods around me as we wandered the store, keeping track of my mom out of the corner of my eye.

Except that the next time I looked up, she was gone! I was all by myself in the busy store. Of course, *she* hadn't lost me. She was just taller than me (at the time) and could see farther. She was a few yards away, examining produce or something. Phew!

That day, all I had lost was the location of my mom for a few minutes. That was scary enough; but there came a point in my sickness where I felt like I had lost so much more: myself. Physically, mentally, emotionally, and even sometimes, spiritually.

***

Fast–forward several years, and this time I was walking around a middle school track with my mom, physically not doing so badly for once. My mind on the other hand . . . something had changed. It felt like Sara had . . . left.

We had finally been settled in our house for two or three months, and outwardly things seemed like they'd begun to calm down. The last year and a half had been crazy—months of no diagnosis, and then the flurry of chaos as we finally did discover what was causing my physical struggles. Multiple unplanned moves, months without a home or a safe place of our own, confusion, and simply put: chaos! We lived in survival mode, taking a deep breath and one thing at a time.

Sure, it was hard and felt traumatic while it was happening, but now that the first few months had passed, things suddenly felt different. We were in it for the long haul. Our lives weren't going to return to normal with this next new treatment—they simply couldn't!

Our lives had changed, our perspectives had changed, and we had changed. I had changed. I didn't know who I was now, only that I wasn't who I was before, and that there would be no getting her back. Even if all of the outward circumstances returned to exactly what they had been on July 22, the day before I got sick those years ago. I was lost.

What was I to do? How did I process everything that had happened —was still happening—and how it all would affect my life for years to come? Walking around that middle school track, I tried to verbalize it all to my mom.

Before I'd gotten sick, I loved to run. Before I'd gotten sick, I used to make jewelry. Before I'd gotten sick, I was reliable, consistent, and in control.

Now, I was fragile, confused, and most of all, I felt lost. Lost in what to do, how to react, and where I was going. I felt like I'd lost . . . *myself.* It felt like everything that was the Sara I had been before was gone. It felt like she had shattered at my feet. Not just chipped, not just broken, but *shattered.* It felt like I had come crumbling violently down.

Even if I someday managed to stand back up again, I knew that pieces of me would be left behind. You can't glue a shattered vase back together and not leave some parts still scattered on the ground. Some pieces are too jagged or sharp to pick back up again, too broken to glue back together, or too small for anyone else to see.

That's a scary feeling—losing yourself (definitely worse than it was in the grocery store years before). You are the thing that you thought you would always have control over. But then when everything that you thought defined you gets ripped away . . . what are you left with?

The thing that I learned (and am still learning) is that none of that stuff before actually *defined* me. Or at least it shouldn't have.

God still loves, and always will love, the shards . . . ugly, broken, and sharp as they may be. He is far greater than any of the things we are facing.

What's My Identity Now?

There's one thing I have that can never be taken away, and that is where my identity *does* rest: God. God's love for me won't change, and my identity in Him shouldn't change. I am a daughter of the King, and nothing can take that away from me.

Who shall separate us from the love of Christ? Shall trouble or hardship or persecution or famine or nakedness or danger or sword? As it is written: "For your sake we face death all day long; we are considered as sheep to be slaughtered." No, in all these things we are more than conquerors through him who loved us. For I am convinced that neither death nor life, neither angels nor

demons, neither the present nor the future, nor any powers, neither height nor depth, nor anything else in all creation, will be able to separate us from the love of God that is in Christ Jesus our Lord.
(Romans 8:35–39)

When all of the things that I thought were who I was before—a runner and a jewelry maker; someone who was emotionally strong and a clear thinker; a good sister, friend, and daughter, etc.—when all that gets torn away, what is left is just me and God.

Part of why that is so scary is because I don't really like the me I see in that. That Sara isn't the goody-two-shoes that she seemed like before. I, and everyone else, get to see just how sinful Sara really is. Just how broken. Just how weak.

The thing is, I've come to realize that this is one of God's biggest gifts to me in this process: learning my weakness. Learning how to rely not on myself, but rather on God. And learning just how amazing God's grace is in light of my exposed sin, motives, and tendencies.

So . . . maybe losing ourselves isn't such a horrible thing. Yes, it hurts. Yes, it's hard. But it's okay if we lose ourselves because we won't lose God.

I have been crucified with Christ and I no longer live, but Christ lives in me. The life I now live in the body, I live by faith in the Son of God, who loved me and gave himself for me.
(Galatians 2:20)

Our identity isn't in ourselves, our sickness, circumstances, or abilities. No, it's in God. We were not created to reflect ourselves but to reflect God.

I was the girl with the chemical filtering mask on. Usually, when we move into a new community (we've moved a good number of times in my life so far), I'm not the family member that everyone knows. That would be my brother. But when we moved to Arizona, it changed. I wore a mask much of the time to protect me from mold

17

and chemical exposure. And people did come to know me as the mask girl. As the sick girl. When they looked at me, they didn't look into my eyes first, they looked at my mask. Everyone was polite and kind, but the mask was—to them—a big part of my identity.

It's easy for sickness to become what we define ourselves by as well. We're the sick girl or guy. Sickness affects so many parts of life in such invasive ways, it begins to feel like it's who we are. Sometimes, it feels natural and practical and is done unconsciously, but it's very easy for that to slip into something unhealthy.

God may use illness to shape us. But it should not define us.

The good news is that even when we lose track of ourselves, God doesn't.

Do you remember the grocery store story? Well, just like my mom hadn't lost track of me, God, our Heavenly Father, hasn't lost track of us. It's all okay because God's got us. (He can see much farther than we can!) Just like we talked about in chapter one, He will never leave us or forsake us.

My flesh and my heart may fail, but God is the strength of my heart and my portion forever. (Psalm 73:26)

We may feel like we've lost ourselves. But in God, we are found, and we are finding Him.

Our Lives Are Not Our Own

Our culture strives toward "self-discovery". It says that we should find, realize, or discover ourselves. But this is the opposite of what God says!

Anyone who loves their life will lose it, while anyone who hates their life in this world will keep it for eternal life. (John 12:25)

Our lives aren't our own! Why in the world should we seek to discover ourselves? When I stop to really think about it, I realize just how self-centered that is. It's us trying to seek to know everything and to be in control of our lives when really, we should be seeking to surrender our lives to God. Just look at this quote by Oswald Chambers in his book *My Utmost for His Highest.*

"Our Lord's teaching was always anti-self-realization. His purpose is not the development of a person—His purpose is to make a person exactly like Himself, and the Son of God is characterized by self-expenditure. If we believe in Jesus, it is not what we gain but what He pours through us that really counts. God's purpose is not simply to make us beautiful, plump grapes, but to make us grapes so that He may squeeze the sweetness out of us."

***

But still, we have the question: Who in the world are we now that all we thought we were is gone? Is my identity now just "the sick kid"? Is yours?

Have you watched the movie *Toy Story*? If you have, you probably remember that there was a guy who had identity struggles too. His name was Buzz Lightyear and he was made of plastic. Guess what though? His friend Woody reminded him who he was . . . or more accurately, *whose* he was—Andy's! Written on the bottom of Buzz's space boots was that name: Andy.

And you also were included in Christ when you heard the message of truth, the gospel of your salvation. When you believed, you were marked in him with a seal, the promised Holy Spirit . . .
(Ephesians 1:13)

Just like Buzz, we are marked. We are marked! We are His! We are not just "the sick kid," no matter how all-consuming our sickness seems to be. We are God's.

So many times, I have cried out to God saying, "I just want my life back!"

I just want my life back. I don't want to have to think about my sickness all the time, evaluating whether I can do something or not, and having to consider how it will affect me since everything causes a chain reaction.

Most people can splurge sometimes, whether it's by allowing themselves a break, going out and doing something fun, or eating junk food. We can't. We don't have that option. We only have so much energy.

We can't escape the constant sickness and thus have a break. If we eat the wrong thing, it could cause days of consequences. If we overwork or overestimate our physical strength, stamina, and ability one day, we can't simply "push through" the next day.

But why would I want my life back? That would mean taking it back from the One who created it! And I would never want to do that. I've already surrendered it into His hands. Let's leave it there! Don't you agree?

Was It Worth It?

The first time I took the Myers-Briggs personality test was after I had been sick for more than a year. Everyone had told me how accurate it was, and I had finally gotten around to taking it. But as I went through the questions, I was suddenly frustrated. As I debated between answers, it turned out to be harder to choose than I imagined. Why? Because for each question, I felt like I had been one way before getting sick, but now I was a different way.

Did I consider myself an introvert or an extrovert? Well, before getting sick, I certainly enjoyed company a lot more than now when I am forced by my sickness to be an introvert. Now, I don't know how the test works, and it may have come out very similarly to how it would have before I got sick, but to me, it was just one more way I saw how I had changed. And I was faced with the question "Was it worth it?"

Around the same time, I decided to change my profile picture on my email and other various accounts. But again, it seemed a lot more emotionally complicated than I ever imagined it would be. It was such a little thing, but to me, it represented more change.

Usually, I'm not the one who dislikes change (that would also be my brother). But my old profile picture was taken on the top of a mountain where we used to live—a place I missed. And it was taken while we were out on a hike—something I could no longer do.

I didn't want to 'let go' of that Sara who used to be. The Sara who could hike up mountains and smile so easily. The one who was happily unaware that the next years of her life would go nothing like what she expected.

Of course, I did change my profile picture, choosing to accept the Sara I had now become. The Sara who was in my eyes weaker and more flawed than she had ever been.

He's Making Diamonds

Which brings to mind the question again: Was it worth it? Have you ever asked yourself that question? I have. Sometimes my answer is a tearful "Yes," and other times it's a form of "I don't know."

Often, I am so thankful that it really isn't up to me to make that choice, and that God is in control. This is His will, and He knows what is best for me.

Guess what? We can *know* that it's worth it. God won't waste our tears or our pain. The title of this book is *He's Making Diamonds*. And He is!

Consider it pure joy, my brothers and sisters, whenever you face trials of many kinds, because you know that the testing of your faith produces perseverance. Let perseverance finish its work so that you may be mature and complete, not lacking anything. (James 1:2–4)

Maybe we are broken. But we are broken so that we can come out stronger. So that we can be shaped more into the image of God. You may have heard the verse that talks about God purifying His people like silver. But how is silver purified? In the fire.

See, I have refined you, though not as silver; I have tested you in the furnace of affliction. For my own sake, for my own sake, I do this. How can I let myself be defamed? I will not yield my glory to another. (Isaiah 48:10–11)

We are hard pressed on every side, but not crushed; perplexed, but not in despair; persecuted, but not abandoned; struck down, but not destroyed. (2 Corinthians 4:8–9)

One day, I compared my life to a Jenga-puzzle (complete with a sort-of-distinguishable-drawing). Blocks of me kept getting yanked out, gently or not-so-gently, and it felt like I was going to topple over. Especially when it came to the more important stabilizing blocks, like, say, mental strength and stability. But there was a bit more to this picture. Yes, blocks were getting taken, but I was also gaining blocks on the top of my tower. And I knew God had His hands around me, steadying the tower and preventing it from falling. All I had to do was trust in Him.

A friend recently told me about her uncle who was a Marine. She told me he said that in training they purposely break you to build you up again, even stronger. God is doing the same thing for us. He's wearing away parts of us: pride, immaturity, etc., and building us up again, in Him, stronger. He's chipping away at the rock concealing the diamond so that the true beauty may be revealed.

Take It Deeper

- In this chapter we talked about identity. We talked about how important it is that we find our identity in God, and how hard it is to not let our sickness define us. Sometimes it's hard to remember who (or rather, whose) you are. If you are having trouble remembering who (or whose) you are, it's good to have a reminder.

- Today I challenge you to write it down on a sticky note or something and put it where you will see it. Maybe just write down a verse from this chapter as a reminder. For example, one day, I was struggling to remember that God's grace and love were sufficient for me and that I was God's child . . . So I put on a cross necklace that I had sitting around as a reminder. I still wear it on days I'm struggling. Reminders you can hold like that can be helpful.

- It's also good to have someone who will remind you who you are when you start to fall into the mindset that your sickness is your identity. Ask someone to help remind you of your true identity when they notice that you are slipping into that mindset by what you say. Make sure it's someone who understands that sickness does have to be considered and remembered, though, and that they won't confuse unhealthy obsession with healthy planning.

- Right now, why don't you pray and tell God all the things you are struggling to adjust to with how illness has shaped and changed you and your life. Surrender it to Him and thank Him that it is all worth it and that His plan is good. Ask Him to help you with your struggles.

S.G. Willoughby

3. The Pit of Despair and the Fight for Joy

"I've been asking these questions, and the answer was here all the time. What is the way? What is the truth? Where is my life? How do I have life living in this? Jesus."
-Sara's journal, November 18, 2017

A cheerful heart is good medicine, but a crushed spirit dries up the bones. -Proverbs 17:22

Somewhere in the middle of our six weeks spent in the state of Montana, my family and I took a weekend and drove to stay at a ski lodge. Not to ski—it wasn't ski season—but just to hang out and get a much-needed break.

It was Mother's Day, and we were exhausted from moving, house building, etc. The lodge had a hot tub and hiking trails, and that was good enough for us! But that vacation wasn't . . . my best. In truth, I think I was just having a two-day pity party. There were lots of tears, moping, and mournful lying around everywhere.

Of course, I did have to miss out on the family hiking adventures. And it made me feel bad to be near the chlorine hot tub, so I missed that too. And I constantly felt like I was going to throw up if I raised my head and wasn't lying down. So, sure, I had excuses. But I also had allowed myself to be dragged down into the pit of despair, even though I know that if I had tried, I could have enjoyed that mini-vacation.

It's so easy to get caught up in our woes, isn't it? I mean, they're right in front of us. In our faces. It's not only that it's easy to get dragged down into them. We actually have to try—hard—to stay out of our woes in an unhealthy way.

Now to be clear, not all sadness is wrong. Far from it! And not all sadness about sickness is wrong either. But that's what we're going to be looking at in this chapter: the good tears, the bad tears, and everything in between.

There is a time for everything, and a season for every activity under the heavens: . . . a time to weep and a time to laugh, a time to mourn and a time to dance . . . (Ecclesiastes 3:1, 4)

Self-Pity

Let's jump right in with a difficult one: self-pity. (I told you it was challenging.) I've struggled with this on numerous occasions, and it is a nasty one to overcome.

The problem with self-pity is that we become so focused on ourselves and what we think our "rights" are that we lose sight of hope, joy, awareness of those around us, and ultimately, God.

Which is a big no-no. We are called to fix our eyes on Jesus!

Therefore, since we are surrounded by such a great cloud of witnesses, let us throw off everything that hinders and the sin that so easily entangles. And let us run with perseverance the race marked out for us, fixing our eyes on Jesus, the pioneer and perfecter of faith. For the joy set before him he endured the cross, scorning its shame, and sat down at the right hand of the throne of God. Consider him who endured such opposition from sinners, so that you will not grow weary and lose heart. (Hebrews 12:1–3)

In other words, self-pity is selfish and self-centered. We are not called to be self-centered. No, we are called to seek to be like Jesus. We are commanded to love.

"A new command I give you: Love one another. As I have loved you, so you must love one another." (John 13:34)

As Jesus has loved us. Jesus loved us by giving up His very life for us on the cross. Jesus loved us by becoming human and coming to earth when He could have stayed in Heaven with God. Jesus loved the crowds that followed Him, stopping to bless little children and heal blind beggars that no one thought He would have any interest in. Jesus loved by pushing through His physical discomfort of exhaustion and emotional discomfort needing time to mourn His cousin, John the Baptist's, death to teach the crowds seeking Him. He put others before Himself. He was *definitely* not self-centered or self-pitying.

While on the cross, Jesus didn't tell the angels at His command to relieve Him. Instead, He took care of His mother, Mary, by assigning a disciple to take care of her, and He asked God to forgive those who had put Him there. Even in His pain and suffering, Jesus was focused on loving those around Him.

Clearly, self-pity is not something we are supposed to indulge in. It is not love. It is not what God has called us to. In fact, He has commanded the opposite. And Jesus has demonstrated the opposite.

I know that doesn't make it easy to do. We are human, and our sinful nature is bent toward ourselves. But in God's grace and mercy, we don't have to live in self-pity. Besides, self-pity simply isn't healthy for us. It prompts us to give up, to lose hope, and leaves us feeling so . . . awful.

One thing to keep in mind, however, is that self-pity is not the same thing as self-mercy. They are two very different things, and self-mercy is as important as self-pity is unhealthy—maybe even more so. We need to learn to have mercy and compassion for ourselves even as we fight self-pity at the same time. But more on mercy later.

In the Bible, there was someone who struggled with self-pity as well. Don't you love how there is always some biblical hero that had the same issues we do? After all, *No temptation has overtaken you except what is common to mankind. And God is faithful; he will not let you be tempted beyond what you can bear. But when you are tempted, he will also provide a way out so that you can endure it.* (1 Corinthians 10:13).

Anyway, this person was living in Israel, which was currently going through a famine. Because of the famine, she and her family decided to move to Moab, a nearby country, where, ideally, there was more food to be had. Can you imagine how hard that must have been? Leaving home and family because of lack of food? I've moved to a new country before . . . it's no piece of cake!

But things got worse for Naomi. (Yes, you guessed it—it was her!) Her husband soon died. The partner of her life, the father of her sons . . . he was gone.

Did she ever heal from that? We don't know. But eventually, things started looking up. Her sons both married devoted, loyal Moabite girls who loved their mother-in-law . . .

Only to have her two sons die as well. If her husband's death hadn't broken her, then surely this did. Can you imagine? All your family dead, and you the only one left. Of course, there were Ruth and Orpah, but somehow, they couldn't fill the void.

Up and down, up and down . . . would Naomi ever have peace? Now she heard that Israel had food again. Would it last? Maybe she could just go home and try to forget about it all. But her daughters-in-law insisted on coming with her. That wouldn't do. She was better off alone. No one else to die, and she could be properly alone to stew in her sadness. So, she tried to send them away.

But Naomi said, "Return home, my daughters. Why would you come with me? Am I going to have any more sons, who could become your husbands? Return home, my daughters; I am too old to have another husband. Even if I thought there was still hope for me—even if I had a husband tonight and then gave birth to sons—would you wait until they grew up? Would you remain unmarried for them? No, my daughters. It is more bitter for me than for you, because the Lord's hand has turned against me!" (Ruth 1:11–13)

Clearly, we don't know all that Naomi was feeling. She had obviously suffered greatly. Her life had been hard. If I had faced what she had, I think I would have broken. And maybe she did break. I know I have no right to say that she should have handled things better or been sweeter. Upon returning to Israel, she told the people to call her Mara (which means "bitter"). She was no longer the same Naomi (which means "pleasantness") they'd known.

Perhaps Naomi was very concerned about her daughters-in-law, trying to do what was best for them and give them what she thought they wanted: freedom from her. But . . . you think she could have been gentler to Ruth and Orpah. They too had lost husbands! Sure, things were perhaps better off for them. At least they had hope of marrying again and starting over. But they were hurting too! It didn't help any of the three that Naomi was comparing her suffering to theirs. To me, she seems focused on herself, not realizing the hurt that her daughters-in-law were also feeling.

Of course, later this changes, as Ruth continues to show her love and compassion at her own expense, and Naomi learns to focus on Ruth's needs too. She finds Ruth an amazing husband and takes care of her. This time it was Ruth in a new country, having left any family, and Naomi became her mother.

It just all comes back to love. Are we loving others? Or are we too focused on ourselves? When we are focused on ourselves, we can't see the need around us. But when we are focused on others, our own pain becomes much less overwhelming. We can only focus on one or the other most at one time.

What Is Joy, and Where Does It Come From?

There's another type of harmful sadness, and it's just as difficult to manage, if not worse. Any guesses? Yep, despair. Despair and depression. In some ways, it's similar to self-pity. It means giving up and allowing ourselves to be enclosed and smothered by a dark cloud.

But . . . it doesn't have to be that way. You see, there's this wonderful thing called joy. Three small letters that can pass as insignificant in the face of the threatening storms, but that are in reality extremely powerful. J-o-y.

I grew up singing "I got the joy, joy, joy, joy down in my heart. Down in my heart to stay!" It's upbeat, simple, and—in my opinion—difficult to sing without smiling. (You just tried, didn't you?) Joy was so simple and easy then. There wasn't anything to get in the way. Sure, I had bad days, but not bad months or bad years. It was easy to smile and laugh and be happy.

But then I got sick. And it was months of unknown, with no diagnosis. All I knew was that my body hurt, and things were harder. Sensory overload took away things like the ability to worship with music. Brain fog took away school, reading, and writing. I couldn't participate in activities with my friends like I used to. I was saddened by eating spinach over and over again for every meal.

Now, looking back, I think, "Those were the days!" Because, of course, things eventually got much worse and much harder. But at the time, it was difficult. I would get discouraged and joy became more of a choice and less of something that appeared to come naturally.

Yes, joy was and is a choice. That's the first thing that we need to know concerning joy. Joy is not the same thing as happiness. Happiness is an emotion. It comes and goes. But if we have joy—true, real joy—it doesn't have to leave. Ever.

So what is joy? If it's not happiness, then what is it? It's not smiling. It's not cheerfulness or laughing. It's not energy. It's not a bubbly personality or making jokes, though all of those things are good. Joy isn't feeling good all the time. It isn't a state of denial, a passing emotion, or about us.

Joy is fixing our eyes on Jesus. It is holding on to Him, trusting Him, and choosing to continue to hope. It is trying our best to "keep our spirits up." To choose not to fall into the pit of despair, no matter how hard it pulls on us. It is hard. It takes a lot of fighting. And on our own, we are incapable of holding on to joy in the valley of death. But God has given us the power to choose joy and to fight for it no matter what. *No matter what.*

I realize it's so much easier said than done. Trust me, I know. And as humans, we sometimes lose the will to hang on to joy. We struggle to force ourselves to have it. Which brings us to the next question: Where does joy come from?

Joy doesn't come from our situation, our circumstances, or the people around us. All of those things will fail. Events will go wrong. People will disappoint us. We'll get sick. Dreams will die. Things will be lost.

Joy also doesn't come from ourselves. We sure aren't strong enough to provide joy for ourselves. We can't generate it out of thin air. We are susceptible to emotions and events. There is only one Person who is steady and dependable no matter what happens, no matter what we—or others—do. There is only One from whom our joy can come.

God.

The Bible says that joy is a fruit of the Spirit (see Galatians 5:22). Joy doesn't come from ourselves, it comes from having the Holy Spirit in our hearts and in our lives.

So he said to me, "This is the word of the Lord to Zerubbabel: 'Not by might nor by power, but by my Spirit,' says the Lord Almighty." (Zechariah 4:6)

There will be times when we simply don't feel like it. When we can't muster up the courage or the energy to pursue joy. What do we do then?

We don't give up. We pray that God would fill our hearts and minds with joy, and then we try our best to smile and be cheerful until the rest of us follows. Even if that just means refraining from complaining and praying that God would make you content. Try your hardest and ask God to help you with the rest. Joy is, like we said before, a choice. That means we choose to *be* joyful even when we don't feel like it. That is the time that joy matters the most: when it's hard.

But What about Depression?

All right, here comes the tricky part. Not that the rest of this chapter has been a piece of cake, but now we're going to address a topic that I confess I'm still trying to figure out: depression. I don't have all the answers. Like I said earlier, things got harder. My original sadness and discouragement eventually gave way to full–on depression . . . and it made me question what joy actually meant. But here's what I've learned.

Despair and depression isn't all . . . circumstantial. It's not all black and white, but more grayish. Some depression is caused by mental illnesses, brain injuries, lack of nutrients for our brains, etc. It's not exactly optional in those cases. So, where does joy fit into *that?*

I've always been taught to be self-controlled when it comes to emotions. But there came a time when I found myself sobbing on the floor, and it felt physically uncontrollable, as if I couldn't stop if I tried. It was just my body's way of handling whatever was going wrong inside it because of illness. Have you been there?

The human spirit can endure in sickness, but a crushed spirit who can bear? (Proverbs 18:14)

The first time I experienced this for myself was just a few days before Christmas in 2016. It brought me staggering to my knees, totally confused. I had no idea what was going on. It felt like a dark, smothering blanket was wrapping around me, tighter and tighter. And then . . . I eventually got a break, and I was able to breathe and see things clearly. The difference was night and day, black and white. One day, the world seemed so, so terrible, and everything seemed hopeless. The next day, it seemed bright and beautiful. It was a mind-shocking experience.

How in the world do we handle such things? How do we handle depression forced on us that isn't really our choice? What is right and wrong in this situation? And if every situation is different, how can there even be basic guidelines or fallbacks?

This was unlike anything I'd experienced before. New territory with no one to tell me how to navigate it. Maybe you've felt or are feeling the same thing. Facing the impossible, how do we find a way out?

The Bible says that we will not be tempted beyond what we can bear and that God will provide a way out (see 1 Corinthians 10:13). But it sure doesn't feel bearable sometimes.

Thankfully, God knows our limits better than we can. And He won't give us too much. He doesn't ask us to do things in obedience to Him that are impossible. Perhaps with us it is impossible, but God isn't limited by the possible. He provides a way. He Himself *is* the way.

Jesus answered, "I am the way and the truth and the life. No one comes to the Father except through me." (John 14:6)

I don't have all the answers. Despite the time I've spent praying and asking what to do with the overwhelming depression that continues to come and go, I still don't feel confident in my conclusions. However, there is One who does have the answers and One whom we can be confident in. He knows what is right, and He has told us what is right in His Word.

When we are too weak, He is strong. We can trust Him when He says that He will always provide a way out. This doesn't mean that we will always do things right. Every time I make it through an episode of depression to the other side, I think, "I'll do better next time." But most of the time, I don't manage to really handle anything better when "next time" rolls around.

We just have to try our best. Our best is enough. There's no such thing as giving 110%. In our weakness, God's grace is sufficient (which we'll discuss more in chapter twelve). Yes, self-control is still a fruit of the Spirit, and yes, we can still choose to have joy and to fight for it—but depression is also a physical thing.

Over and over again, I had to choose to have mercy on myself when I simply wasn't strong enough to have the smile and happiness that I thought I should have all the time.

Hang on! Keep fighting. I know it's hard. And sometimes we slip and fall. But when you face depression, simply try to look at Jesus. Try to ignore the waves tossing you everywhere and keep looking at your Savior.

There are no easy answers, but as someone once said, "If you can't run toward Jesus, walk, and if you can't walk, then crawl, and if all you can do is lay there and look in Jesus' direction, that's enough." Rely on God. He won't leave you in the pit of despair. He will provide a way out. He will help you to avoid sinning. He will help you overcome the lies.

Why? Because He loves you.

Who among you fears the Lord and obeys the word of his servant? Let the one who walks in the dark, who has no light, trust in the name of the Lord and rely on their God. (Isaiah 50:10)

Choosing to Look for Blessings

Have you ever read Psalm 77? Yes? No? All right, well, either way, go read it now if you have a moment.

Did you do it? Yeah, I didn't think so. (If you did, extra imaginary cookies for you!) Let me give you an overview of it for a moment.

The psalm starts out with the writer, Asaph, listing his woes. He talks about groaning, not being comforted, lacking sleep, and being too troubled to speak. When we get to verses 7–9, he says this:

"Will the Lord reject forever? Will he never show his favor again? Has his unfailing love vanished forever? Has his promise failed for all time? Has God forgotten to be merciful? Has he in anger withheld his compassion?"

He's pretty upset. It sounds like he's given up hope, right? But the very next verses hold an important key.

Then I thought, "To this I will appeal: the years when the Most High stretched out his right hand. I will remember the deeds of the Lord; yes, I will remember your miracles of long ago. I will consider all your works and meditate on all your mighty deeds."

The rest of the psalm is filled with Asaph remembering what God has done for him in the past. He purposely and consciously lists everything, choosing to dwell on God's past working in his life, and choosing to trust God's power to work in his life again.

I challenge you to do the same thing. Write them down. Or, if your body hurts too much for you to write, then verbally thank God for all that He has done in your life already. It's okay if you have brain fog that jumbles your words or makes it hard to make sense. God knows what you are saying—just say it!

Maybe it seems hard right now to look for blessings. Maybe your pain is clouding your thinking, or your trials are obscuring your view. Maybe when you stop and think, all that comes to mind are the hard things that God has given you. The things that you aren't so sure you want. Then choose to thank Him for those things.

However, if you look, really choose to look, then I'm sure you will find things in your life, whether it's things in the past or things now —I'm sure you can find something to praise God for. It's like some sort of *Where's Waldo?* book, except better. Surely our King's gifts are even greater rewards to look for than finding a candy cane sweater.

If you, then, though you are evil, know how to give good gifts to your children, how much more will your Father in heaven give good gifts to those who ask him! (Matthew 7:1)

Make a list of the people whose lives have been touched through your sickness. Have you gained a better understanding of other people's sufferings? Thank Him. Do you see how He worked out a situation that would have been hard to handle? Thank Him.

For example, there are many dear friends of mine that I never would have met if God hadn't brought me to where I needed to be *through my trials* so that I was in a position to meet them.

And yes . . . thank God for your sickness and your trials.

I know how impossible and difficult that is to hear. It's really hard for me to say, trust me.

But thank Him for what He has done in your life through the sickness He has put there. Do you remember what I said in chapter one about this sickness being a gift allowed by God? That it was an expression of His love to us?

Well, what do you do when you get a gift? When I get a gift from my grandparents, I usually make a thank you card out of ribbon and paper and mail it to them. When I get a gift from my family, I might give them a hug. When God gives us a gift, we should thank Him.

Right now, you may resent His gift. It sure doesn't look like much of a gift a lot of the time, right? But it's what He has given us for this season of our lives, and He isn't going to apologize for it. (Who apologizes for giving a gift when they know the receiver needs it?)

When we talk about joy, we need to realize it isn't optional. Over and over again in the Bible joy is a clear command. Just look at 1 Thessalonians 5:16–18: *Rejoice always, pray continually, give thanks in all circumstances; for this is God's will for you in Christ Jesus.*

One thing I especially like about that and other verses is the word 'rejoice'. *Re*-joice. Remember again the things God has already done, remember again His past faithfulness, and don't lose hope for His present faithfulness. And keep doing it. Keep rejoicing in what He has done.

In 1 Corinthians 6, Paul speaks about being sorrowful, yet always rejoicing. I was listening to a sermon by John Piper, and he made a great point. The opposite of joy is not suffering. It's not. The opposite of joy is despair.

Suffering can even *foster* joy if we allow it. Suffering rips away all of the false happiness that we think is joy and allows us to learn the hard lesson that joy is not a general thing. Our joy is not in our circumstances, not in the people around us, and not in our health. It's in our amazing God. *That* is where this joy comes from. Pursue God and choose to delight in Him and joy will follow. It will be hard, yes. But joy comes from Him!

In light of all that, then, let's learn to trust God's future gifts and blessings, to look for His gifts and blessings now and thank Him, and to remember His working in our life previously. Let us learn to view our sickness as a gift. Learn to thank Him for it from our hearts.

Rejoice in the Lord always. I will say it again: Rejoice!
(Philippians 4:4)

Two Ways to Fight for Joy

So many worship songs and Bible verses talk about joy being a strength. And it is! Joy is a strength like no other. Fear or despondency won't give us strength. Joy will. But sometimes, it feels like it takes all my strength just to have joy in the first place.

So, what exactly is it that helps us have joy? Jesus is the way out of depression and the Holy Spirit is the One who gives us joy. But . . . what are we supposed to *do*? Joy doesn't come from us. But what does it come from? God, for sure, but how do we pursue joy?

If joy isn't something that just drops into our lap, but something we have to seek and fight for . . . how do we seek it or fight for it?

The secret is actually a discipline we've already touched on: gratitude. Thankfulness. Choosing—as we've already established—to *look* for blessings, consciously thanking God for the life He has given us. James 1:2-4 says,

Consider it pure joy, my brothers and sisters, whenever you face trials of many kinds, because you know that the testing of your faith produces perseverance. Let perseverance finish its work so that you may be mature and complete, not lacking anything.

Consider it pure joy. Consider, ponder, think. Stop and think about how thankful you are for your trials. Think about all of the good things that have come because of them. I know it hurts. It's hard. It's not easy. But we are commanded to *consider it pure joy*. Not just joy . . . *pure* joy. Real, dependable, raw joy. Yet again, it's thankfulness. It's fixing our eyes on Jesus, not ourselves.

I used to make pickles. We had these thirty-two-ounce jars and they would *just* fit two layers of cucumber slices (if we cut them correctly and packed them tightly enough). Then we'd mix the seasonings, herbs, etc., and put them in on top. Next, we'd fill it with water; that way the seasonings would eventually fall to the bottom. Finally, we'd close the lid (tightly) and shake so that it all got fully coated. If you're making the large batches that we did (our garden was prolific . . . well, the cucumbers were), then you can hand a jar or two to your brother and his friends to shake for a while. It's easier that way.

After that, it's all about waiting the four to seven days for them to be properly pickled.

Why am I telling you this? Because making pickles is a process, just like this verse says that faith is a process. Producing something doesn't happen immediately. It takes work and effort and time and tears. But the result is homemade pickles versus store-bought ones.

Why should we consider it pure joy? Because the testing of faith produces perseverance. Then we will be mature and complete, not lacking anything.

So then, what's the second way we can fight for joy? I'll give you a hint: expressing thanks to God is a part of it.

It's prayer. The first way to fight for joy is thankfulness, and the second way to fight for joy is through prayer. What did Jesus do when He was overwhelmed with sorrow? He prayed.

"My soul is overwhelmed with sorrow to the point of death," he said to them. "Stay here and keep watch." Going a little farther, he fell to the ground and prayed that if possible the hour might pass from him. "Abba, Father," he said, "everything is possible for you. Take this cup from me. Yet not what I will, but what you will."
(Mark 14:34–36)

Jesus brought His sorrow to God and God gave Him the strength to make it through the trials and suffering before Him. If we look ahead to verse 38, it says,

"Watch and pray so that you will not fall into temptation. The spirit is willing, but the flesh is weak."

Watch and pray. Maybe we want joy. We want to delight in God. But we are too weak. Fighting for joy is hard. So we pray. We fight for it by asking God to fight for us. Yet again, I think of 1 Thessalonians 5:16–18. That passage of Scripture is really the summary of what this chapter is about:

Rejoice always, pray continually, give thanks in all circumstances; for this is God's will for you in Christ Jesus.

Rejoice.

Pray.

Give thanks.

Why? Because it's God will for us... in Christ Jesus. Not through ourselves, but through the power that Jesus gives us.

That is how we fight for joy.

The Good Kind of Sad

"I will not say: do not weep; for not all tears are an evil."
-Gandalf the Grey

Not all tears and sadness are bad though. Even Jesus wept! And we all know He was perfect, so that means being sad isn't a sin. God made tears for a reason. Let's take a moment to talk about tears, so it's beneficial to have a good grasp of their importance. We all have them from time to time. It's okay to be having a rough day or month. It's okay to find yourself at the end of your rope. Franklin Delano Roosevelt once said, "When you reach the end of your rope, tie a knot in it and hang on." But so often I feel like I don't even have the strength to tie a knot. And that's okay! Just throw yourself on Jesus when you get to the end of your rope.

Tears are healthy a lot of the time. It's okay to be weak. It's okay to cry. There were a few months when I would make it through each day, only to close my door at night and go to my knees and cry. It was okay. It was part of what kept me going. It's okay to spend that time crying your heart out without anyone else but you and God.

The Lord is close to the brokenhearted and saves those who are crushed in spirit. (Psalm 34:18)

It's also okay to mourn the things that you miss, or that you've lost. Just as long as you don't get sucked in too far and get lost in despair or self-pity. We can't forget to live now, but it's also okay to miss things that we used to be able to do. It's okay to miss your health! Just don't forget to fight for joy and keep your eyes fixed on Jesus. Don't forget to fight the battles that are in front of you now because you are so distracted by the past.

It's actually very important to allow yourself to mourn and lament the things that you have lost. We need to process the things we've lost and the things we have gone through if we are ever going to heal. Emotional, mental, and spiritual healing is just as important as physical healing.

Bringing our brokenness and losses to God is the way to heal. If we try to ignore them or brush them off, they will only fester and weigh us down. Why carry these burdens when we can put them down? When there is One who will carry them for us?

Surely he took up our pain and bore our suffering, yet we considered him punished by God, stricken by him, and afflicted. But he was pierced for our transgressions, he was crushed for our iniquities; the punishment that brought us peace was on him, and by his wounds we are healed. We all, like sheep, have gone astray, each of us has turned to our own way; and the Lord has laid on him the iniquity of us all. (Isaiah 53:4–6)

One day, I read some wise advice. This person told me to write out everything I had lost because of sickness.

I filled a page.

And, I realized that all of the things I had written down weren't my things in the first place. They were God's. And I also realized that losing some of these things wasn't so bad, because it forced me to rely on God, not myself.

The thing about mourning losses from chronic illness is that I'm still figuring out if it ever ends. Things are definitely easier now than they were earlier now that I've purposely brought some of the things to God and processed them.

But there are still things that hurt, things that I still feel the loss of every day. Chronic illnesses generally don't end (at least not quickly), which means that the losses don't end either.

So let me say it again: it's okay, healthy, and even necessary to mourn the things that illness has stolen from us. In fact, there's an entire book about it by Esther Smith that I recommend titled *When Chronic Pain & Illness Take Everything Away: How to Mourn Our Losses*. We just don't want to let it suck us into self-pity and despair.

Sorrow and joy can coexist, after all! (See 2 Corinthians 6:10.)

I remember my affliction and my wandering, the bitterness and the gall. I well remember them, and my soul is downcast within me. Yet this I call to mind and therefore I have hope: Because of the Lord's great love we are not consumed, for his compassions never fail. They are new every morning; great is your faithfulness. (Lamentations 3:19–23)

Take It Deeper

- In this chapter, we talked about a huge topic: joy. We talked about how important it is that we remember to rejoice, choose thankfulness, and depend on God to help us stay joyful, even when our situations make it tough. Joy is something that we need to keep a hold of. But sometimes, that's just hard to do. I said before not to take my words blindly, but to search the Bible for yourself. In many cases, letting God's Word minister to you is the best way to sustain your joy.

- I've compiled a list of Scriptures that pertain to joy and thankfulness. That way you can turn to it whenever you need a jump start in joy and thankfulness. It's not nearly exhaustive, there are just so many! But here are some verses to get you started:

- **Verses about Rejoicing:** 2 Corinthians 1:10–11, 1 Chronicles 16:9–36, Psalm 51:8, Psalm 32:11

- **Verses about Joy & Thankfulness:** Colossians 1:9–13, 1 Thessalonians 5:16–18

- **Verses about the Joy Found in God:** John 15:11, Psalm 86:1–4, Psalm 16:11

- Nothing encourages joyfulness more than thankfulness. So here's your assignment: Write down everything that you are thankful for. Write down things both sickness and non-sickness related. If writing is too hard, do it verbally, or mentally. Keep a running list in your journal, or on sticky notes stuck where you can see them. Choose to rejoice in God's working in the past. Thank Him for the present. And thank Him for whatever plans He has in store for your future. Choose to delight in God and praise Him in the storm.

S.G. Willoughby

4. Communication in Chronic Illness

"How are you?"

"I'm all right, how are you?"

"I'm good."

(Awkward pause)

"So how are you—*really*?"

"Ummm . . ."

Ever been there? When you're sick, or someone you know is sick, life is a constant roller coaster, and that question seems impossible to answer even on a normal day. Don't you think? I mean, even before I got sick, it just seemed to be polite, nonsense words exchanged that didn't really mean anything.

But then you get to the "really?" question and someone actually wants to know how you're holding up. Sometimes that makes me feel like a deer in the headlights. How much time do you have? How much does someone even want to know? How much do you want to verbalize in that moment? How are you anyway? There's a lot of bad, but there's some good in there too . . .

Or what about when they ask you how you feel? Besides the constant ups and downs that make a one-word explanation impossible, this question can get tiring. After all, there *is* more to you than just your sickness, however all-consuming the illness seems. So many emotions and frustrations and dilemmas concerning relationships in the midst of illness go far beyond simple conversation specifics. So, let's get into it!

I suppose we should answer the conversation question before moving on to the deeper, harder stuff. When you've been sick for a long time, sometimes you just want to get out with other people and try to forget everything for a while. So, when they ask the question "How are you?" all the pain rushes in because you can't say a simple thing like "I'm good. I really am good." It hurts.

Other times, all we want is for someone to ask, "How are you?" so that we can finally just get everything off our chest to someone who really wants to hear. Sometimes we want that person to simply listen sympathetically, and other times, we want them to give us answers and help us fix it.

Most of the time, we don't even know what we want, and we're somewhere in the middle. Which is hard enough for us, but what about for those around us? It isn't fair, and it isn't their fault that they can't figure out how to treat us or what we want in each moment.

Besides, even though we could list some guidelines for them, it isn't our job to change them, but rather to figure out how to deal with ourselves. (But don't worry. For those of you who aren't sick and do want to understand us a little better, I'll include some dos and don'ts for you at the end of this chapter out of common request. Sorry we're so confusing.)

Here are my thoughts. No matter what the situation, or what we—or they—do or don't do, God has called us to love those around us. Our conversations should be full of grace and seasoned with salt *so that we may know how to answer everyone* (see Colossians 4:6). That's far easier said than done.

Now, the context of this verse talks about sharing God's truth with outsiders and making the most of every opportunity in wisdom. I think that can definitely apply here as well, but I want to focus specifically on verse six, paraphrased above.

Full of grace. No matter what people say to us. So many times, people make assumptions, misunderstand, and just don't get what we're feeling, thinking, or going through—all the while thinking that they *do* understand.

Even as someone who has been sick for a long time (or short, depending on your point of view), I say the wrong things to people who are in almost exactly the same situation I'm in. I assume that since I've been where they are, I know the things to say.

I want so desperately to share what I think is the truth or comforting words they need to hear when really all I was supposed to do is listen and obey God's prompting. If it isn't His will for me to be the one to share a particular truth that He taught me in similar situations, then I have to accept that. Have you done similar things?

When people say the wrong things to us, it's important to remember that *we* don't always say the right things either. We need to learn to respond with grace and mercy. Most of the time when people say the wrong things, it's really because they're just trying to help or comfort us. They don't know that it hurts.

Of course, that doesn't make things easier to respond to. It doesn't satisfy our need to share our hearts or have comfort and support. When humans fail us, where do we go?

It is better to take refuge in the Lord than to trust in humans. It is better to take refuge in the Lord than to trust in princes.
(Psalm 118:8–9)

We go to God! We're never too much for Him to handle. He's never too busy, too tired, or too stressed out. He's our rock. And you know what? He understands us too! He made us.

Even youths grow tired and weary, and young men stumble and fall; but those who hope in the Lord will renew their strength. They will soar on wings like eagles; they will run and not grow weary, they will walk and not be faint.
(Isaiah 40:30–31)

So, how do we answer the intimidating "How are you?" question? Gracefully and mercifully. Really, it's up to you. There's no magical formula.

Sometimes, it's okay to smile and nod. Especially if there's not the time to explain fully anyway, or you know that the person doesn't really want to know. Sometimes, it's easier to just say something about a particular symptom rather than how you *really* are. That's okay. Be wise. Do your best to discern what matters, if you should share or not, and what's healthy to share or not.

On the other hand, don't be afraid of sharing when God leads you to. It's unhealthy to isolate yourself. We were not created to be alone, and we need to let down our walls and let people in. We need support. We need fellowship.

Sometimes, all we need is a hug. And that's okay. It's okay—necessary, even—to let others in, and allow your weaknesses and struggles to be seen.

What we have to share may be exactly what someone else needs to hear . . . and we may never even find out about it. Our stories are not our own, and God has called us to share our testimonies, to share what He is doing in our lives.

They triumphed over him by the blood of the Lamb and by the word of their testimony; they did not love their lives so much as to shrink from death. (Revelation 12:11)

Let the redeemed of the Lord tell their story—those he redeemed from the hand of the foe . . . (Psalm 107:2)

My mouth will tell of your righteous deeds, of your saving acts all day long—though I know not how to relate them all. (Psalm 71:15)

To Speak or Not to Speak

When speaking about chronic illness—and specifically *your* chronic illness—it's wise to think about when the right time (or reason) might be to talk about it. For example, we don't want to shame someone by belittling their headache that for them is really difficult, just because we think we've had worse.

But it's good to talk about it sometimes. One good reason to talk about illness is to raise awareness. Many people with illness turn out to become the biggest advocates for their sickness. We are the ones frequently raising awareness for those illnesses because we are the ones who understand illness intimately . . . and more than that, we are the ones who see all the misconceptions so many people have.

Speaking about our illness helps others to know that they are not alone and that such things as illness are out there. It helps people know how to avoid those illnesses and help those who have them. And it helps people to *understand*. After all, it's rather difficult to help someone if you don't understand anything about what they are facing.

When I got sick, we didn't even realize that mold poisoning existed like that. But having people speak about it has helped others realize the cause of their illness.

If we are talking about our illness simply to rant or vent or complain on social media for all the world to see and that's *all* we talk about, then it might be time to reevaluate. It's okay to talk about illness. After all, it's a huge part of your life. And it's okay to vent to trusted friends when you need to. It's okay to tell people that you are struggling and to ask for prayer or help. But if all you ever talk about is how miserable your life is, then maybe stop for a moment and ask about other people's lives too. Or when you share your struggle, also try to share a bit of what God is teaching you.

You don't have to be bubbly and "fine" all the time. But share your heart and your struggles in the proper place and at the proper time to the proper people. Sometimes for me, that means writing a blog post about the fact that I'm finding it hard to hope and submitting it to a big website. Other times for me that means calling one of my best friends, spilling it all (or only part of it), and asking her not to talk about it with anyone else. Still other times, it means going on a walk by myself and giving everything to God and God alone.

Be Careful Who You Listen To

As you know, everyone has some opinion or something to say when it comes to illness: doctors who each have a different diagnosis (or none at all); friends who want to recommend all sorts of remedies; people who want to tell us exactly what we are doing right or wrong; fellow illness-warriors who have their own set of suggestions and tips.

Some of those people, opinions, and information are correct. Others are incorrect. And many are somewhere in between. Who do we listen to? Clearly, we can't listen to all of them. After all, many of them contradict each other! On the other hand, it's easy to be overwhelmed and want to curl in a ball, cover our ears, and sing— ignoring all of it.

Neither of which is the most helpful option. Which is why we need to be aware and discerning. We need to be wise about whose advice we take. We need to pray about where God is guiding us, and to whom and what He may be leading us to. He alone knows what is best, He alone knows exactly what we need.

And remember . . . sometimes it's okay to just smile and nod. You don't have to do something just because it's suggested, and we don't want to get stuck on one thing.

As teenagers with chronic illness, we are in a unique position. We are not adults, but we *are* the ones in our bodies, and we have to deal with the consequences of decisions made about our health.

We need to trust God to work through our parents or legal guardians. We can ask to be a part of the decision-making process, but right now they have authority over us, and we can trust God to work through them.

A Fine Art

Communication has personally been one of my biggest struggles. At the best of times communication is a fine art, but at the worst—it can cause problems.

For me this often related closely to the mental struggles that came from my sickness: brain fog, anxiety, depression, etc. I even found that I had developed mental roadblocks against certain simple things.

The best thing that I can say here is to do your best and to pray. As with other things, have mercy on yourself when you're struggling. And ask for mercy from those around you. If you explain what's going on, I've found that most people are very understanding. It just requires us to swallow our pride and explain.

However, do your best. Try to push yourself especially in this area as relationships are so important. Remember also that some people won't understand. Even if we explain it to them, and they smile and nod, they won't understand that many of our miscommunications aren't our choice.

This is where prayer comes in. Cover all of your relationships with prayer, asking God to preserve and protect them even when you're struggling. Pray that God would allow you to be able to do or say the things that you need to.

One more tip is to ask for help from others about communicating. More than once I've brought a phone to my mom with a text or email pulled up and asked her what I should say or to read over the reply I had written, just to make sure it all made sense or came across correctly.

Just Communicate

I just said that the best thing to do when communication is hard because of illness-related mental struggles is to pray. And I stand by that. But as a friend pointed out, just communicate! I know that it seems impossible, and sometimes might *be* impossible. But just try.

This is especially important when you have depression or anxiety. It will be different for each person, but often it is harder to deal with alone. When you bring it into the light and ask for help, it can stop the seemingly never-ending spiral.

I say that with caution, however, because I know that if a person reacts badly, it can make things worse. So communicate. Just do it. Take two minutes or twenty seconds and start speaking—but do so with wisdom. Carefully choose someone you trust to be the person you spill it to first.

Do We Need to Apologize for What Our Mental Illness "Made" Us Say?

Often, I think the mental aspects of illness are the worst. At least, in my opinion, they're the worst. And they mess up a lot of things in normal, day-to-day life.

Especially communication. It's hard to read body language when you have brain fog, hard to figure out how someone really feels about something, or what they're really saying. It's hard to remember things—even important things—in your family's and friends' lives. It's hard to remember people's names. It's hard to understand what's going on around you or remember what you were going to say in the first place. Sometimes you even say things (or not say things) that seriously hurt other people without even realizing it! It's horrible.

Even worse, though, is when you have to deal with the irrational part of mental illness. When it causes you to be anxious, depressed, irrationally irritable, or angry (aka the Hulk), things come out of your mouth that you would never have verbalized otherwise. Eeek!

Now what?

Well, here comes the tricky part. There's a fine line where on one side the Bible calls us to self-control, and on the other side, this is an illness, and we need to show ourselves some mercy. And this illness isn't our fault. This is a very difficult question that I'm still figuring out. But for now, let's look at the question of whether or not we need to apologize for what our illness made us say.

For ourselves, we know that it was in part caused by our illness, and we can't be trapped by guilt, but the thing is, other people don't see it that way. Other people around us can't see the intense battle in our minds. And so when we say things that hurt, it isn't easy for them to understand that it is not us, not what we would say, and not even what we believe to be true. They can't see that and so what we say hurts them. They don't realize that we don't *actually* believe it's true when we're in our right mind.

So, my answer would be yes. Yes, we need to apologize. We need to acknowledge to them that what we said was wrong. We need to have mercy on ourselves and not be trapped by guilt. But we need to help those around us understand that we didn't mean to hurt them and that even though sometimes we couldn't help it, we are sorry we did hurt them. In Numbers 15 God actually addresses unintentional sins for the Israelite community. He says,

"'Now if you as a community unintentionally fail to keep any of these commands the Lord gave Moses—any of the Lord's commands to you through him, from the day the Lord gave them and continuing through the generations to come—and if this is done unintentionally without the community being aware of it, then the whole community is to offer a young bull for a burnt offering as an aroma pleasing to the Lord, along with its prescribed grain offering and drink offering, and a male goat for a sin offering. The priest is to make atonement for the whole Israelite community, and they will be forgiven, for it was not intentional and they have presented to the Lord for their wrong a food offering and a sin offering. The whole Israelite community and the foreigners residing among them will be forgiven, because all the people were involved in the unintentional wrong. (Numbers 15:22–26)

Of course, since Jesus died for our sins we can simply ask forgiveness, and we don't need to sacrifice any animals. But God has told us to be holy. And in our relationships with other people, we want to make things right even if we unintentionally hurt them. That means we not only ask God for forgiveness, we ask them for forgiveness too.

For your close friends and family who will see you in that mental place often, one other thing that can help is to talk to them before you get to that place and tell them about what you are struggling with, and how you don't mean to hurt them. That can help in communication and understanding, and lead to a whole lot less hurt all around. That way, instead of being afraid to hurt them, you can know that they will have your back and that they can help you when you are in that bad place mentally.

The Promised Dos and Don'ts

All right, here it is. Thanks for holding tight! If you're not sick, you've probably wondered how to ask someone how they are in a way that shows you mean it.

For the first few months after getting sick, my illness was still relatively new for me and all those around me, and I was constantly being asked how I was by people who really wanted to know. At first, I appreciated it, but eventually, I got rather tired of the question, and often it was too overwhelming to answer. (It still is—see earlier section.)

However, I've found that it's generally better if you keep asking. Just be willing to be patient with us if we give long, complicated answers or short, vague ones. We may be still figuring things out.

Just keep gently showing us that you love, that you're there when we're ready, and that you won't disappear. Here are some dos and don'ts to think through in the meantime:

Don't ask:

- If you don't really want to know.

- In a crowd. One–on–one is generally better.

- In passing. Most of our answers will probably take time. (Besides the vague confused ones of course.)

- Only about sickness. Remember that we do have other things in our lives besides being sick. Yes, being sick will affect those things, but if you only ask about what foods we can eat, it can get rather depressing for both of us.

- If you can't handle the answer. Our answers may be messy both physically and emotionally.

- If your first response will be to suggest a magical cure. For example, we're so glad that vitamin D helped your cousin, but yes, we are already taking it (and a bunch of other supplements). Not that we won't accept suggestions! Just maybe that shouldn't be your first response when you don't know the full situation and haven't researched our illness extensively yet.

Do ask:

- If you are ready to truly listen, *remember* what we say, and have time enough to hear.

- Educated questions. When you've done even a quick Google search of word definitions to understand what we're talking about, it means a lot and makes it easier for us. It also means you are more likely to believe us. Be willing, though, to learn that your research or conclusions were incorrect. Chronic illnesses are complicated, even for us.

- How you can pray for us.

- Rather than assume. Especially if you're trying to do something for us. (Thanks, by the way!)

Take It Deeper

- Communication is very important. But as we've discussed in this chapter, it's not always easy. Sometimes it doesn't work right, and we get hurt, or we hurt someone. But that doesn't mean we have to give up. We simply need to learn how to forgive, be forgiven, and try again.

- If anyone has hurt you by things they have said or not said, choose right now to forgive them. Say the words "God, I forgive them for [whatever it is]." Yes, even if they haven't apologized. Also think of anyone you might have hurt intentionally or unintentionally and do your best to make things right.

- Now even if there isn't any resentment or unforgiveness, having a good conversation can still be hard. Sometimes just thinking ahead of time about how you might answer, exploring possible ways a conversation could go, can be helpful. You could save yourself some headache. So here's your assignment: Think about questions that you are asked frequently but never know how to reply to. Then think of some general, kind answers that you could use next time you're asked them. If you're stuck, ask someone that you trust for help.

5. Relationships in Chronic Illness

God has blessed me with an amazing family and group of friends who are my support system. Even so, there are still bumps in the road, whether it's because of things other people have done (or not done) or things I've done (or not done). Maybe you have a support system too (whether it's great or not-so-great), or maybe you don't. We'll be addressing both in this chapter.

Grace and the "Bad Friend, Bad Sister, Bad Daughter" Routine

One time, someone close to me was upset about how my illness was affecting their life. And though they hadn't yet said it outright, they were blaming me. It was all my fault. Someone else in the room joked, "What, do you think she's licking mold off the walls or something? Giggling and excited that she's ruining your life?" Everyone laughed, including me.

But the person in question pouted. "Yes, that's what she's doing." Later, that person again repeated the belief. And I don't know if they realized it, but that hurt me. Badly. Since then, I've chosen to forgive them. But they thought it was my fault. And so did I.

This is something I struggle with *a lot*. Especially when I'm not doing well mentally. I hate to be the reason my siblings' Christmas presents are in the garage because the chemicals in them make me sick if they come in the house. It hurts when I don't get to go on family outings and be with them. I hate that I can do next to no chores for a crazy list of reasons and that my siblings have to do it all for me.

I struggle, feeling like a bad friend when most of the time it's me asking for support and never giving it in return. Relationships are supposed to be two-way! I feel so guilty when it takes me forever to answer an email because of my brain fog. I struggle when I can't remember my friends' birthdays or when I miss social cues other people would have gotten. (Oh. I wasn't supposed to mention that? Sorry!) I want to be reliable like I used to be! Don't you?

Something God has been continually teaching me is this amazing, wonderful thing called *grace*. And that it's okay to accept grace and mercy, unconditional and undeserved love. In fact, we *need* to learn to accept it.

I've been taught about unconditional love since I was born. I've heard the Gospel over and over again and repeated it to others over and over again. But when God gave me another way to learn it—through my own helplessness and need for others—it was really hard!

Suddenly, it was more than a spoken truth; it became one I was living—one that I was *receiving*. For me, it was hard simply because of my pride and my desire to be doing it in reverse.

But for others I know it's hard in a completely different way. It's hard to trust because trust has been broken. People have disappeared somewhere in chaos, or worse. But that brings us back to the point before: grace. Just like in everyday conversation, we have to learn to forgive people and trust in God. He will never leave. I know that's easier said than done. I know. But God has commanded it of us, and in His power it's possible.

Now, about the "bad friend, bad sister, bad daughter" thing (or whatever it is for you). God has given you your sickness, right? It's not your fault or something that you chose. Well, God may have given it to more people than just you. Your sickness is a trial to other people in your life, right? It inevitably affects people other than just you. But that isn't your fault.

Do not fall into the trap of guilt—that's from Satan, not from God. If God is convicting you of something, then repent and move on. Be forgiven! But continuing guilt, especially guilt over something that isn't your fault, is wrong. Don't allow yourself to be entrapped by it and get stuck.

Godly sorrow brings repentance that leads to salvation and leaves no regret, but worldly sorrow brings death.
(2 Corinthians 7:10)

Just like God is using your sickness to make a diamond out of you, He may also be using it to shape those He has put in your life, whether it's your family, friends, caregiver, or someone else.

Learn to give yourself grace as well as to accept it from others. Learn that you don't have to be the perfect friend, sibling, or child. Try your best not to let yourself use your sickness as an excuse to treat those around you poorly. But if you're doing your best, and you don't have power over things—then let those things be, okay? And remember, you're learning. Learning takes time. It's okay if you don't master this instantly. It's *okay*.

It's Okay to Be a Burden

One of my biggest fears in my sickness is that I will be a burden. And the truth is, I *am* a burden. It's not something I can avoid. And you know what? That's okay. It's okay to have to rely on other people. It's okay to burden.

Let's stop and identify "burden" for a moment. Because it's okay to be a burden as long as it's the right *type* of burden and as long as you have the right understanding of it. It's not okay to be a burden if you think that means you are useless.

Because news flash: you are not useless. God created you for a purpose and if that's only to lie in bed and pray, that's fine. But thinking of yourself as useless is not fine. God did not create you useless. He created you to be His child. He created you to love, and let me tell you, it is possible to love even if you can't do anything typical to show it. He created you to seek Him, and you can definitely do that from bed.

Being a burden is not okay if you are doing it to manipulate others and to get them to do things for you that you can very well do yourself. If you are truly chronically ill however (even if no one believes you), then I highly doubt that you are doing that.

Being a burden is humiliating, I know. It's hard to be the one that makes life difficult and hard for others. It's hard to see them hurting because of us. But again, if it's not our fault that we are sick, then we shouldn't feel guilty.

Like I said before: this illness may not be only your trial to seek God through. God may be giving it to you for the growth of those around you as well. Galatians 6:2 says:

Carry each other's burdens, and in this way you will fulfill the law of Christ.

Concerning Caregivers

Whining. Complaining. Demanding. Self-centered. Difficult. Hard to please. We all know how to be bad patients. When you have a chronic illness, one of the most important (and probably most difficult) relationships in your life is the one with your caregiver.

With all that you go through together, you're also pretty close—you're forced to be! I don't know who your caregiver is—maybe it's your parent, a sibling, or someone else altogether. Maybe it's a team of people. Maybe, if you're an adult, it's your spouse. For me, it's my mom.

Before we get into this, let me just say that my mom is pretty awesome. She's so strong, very practical, but also flexible. She's an amazing caregiver. I don't know what any of us would do without her, or how we would have survived (or continue surviving) chronic illness.

Caregivers do so much . . . they bravely tackle disgusting tasks and exhausting ones. They get up with us in the night, they go with us to doctor's appointments, and they help us sort out what in the world the new symptom is. They love us, even when we're at our worst, and they serve us constantly, even when there is no end in sight, even when we don't thank them. When no one thanks them. When their needs are overlooked by friends and family because our needs are more blatant.

If you're reading this book, it's likely because either you are sick or someone you know and love is sick. If you are a caregiver, please know that you are amazing. You're a superhero. You *are* loved and appreciated even if all we do is complain. Your battles are just as huge and overwhelming as ours are, except that fewer people see them. Don't get discouraged. You will never know how much you are appreciated or how much what you do means to the person you are taking care of. Because what you do can't be acknowledged by a simple "thank you."

Now, while my mom is amazing, and we were best friends even before I got sick, all relationships have bumps in the road, and this is no exception. Not only do caregivers see us at *our* worst, but we also probably see them at *their* worst, even if they try and hide it from us. So, let's talk about five keys in this crucial relationship.

Five Keys in the Caregiver-Patient Relationship (For the Patient)

1. Continual, unending grace and mercy—the kind that comes only from God. I'm certain that I've been on the receiving end of this one far more than the giving end. One night my mom had just finished giving me my nightly essential oil massage, for my intense joint pain during that time, and had gone to start an Epsom salt bath for me while I let it soak in. It was cold and my body was in so

61

much pain. I didn't think that my mom—or anyone for that matter—*understood.*

I just wanted her to understand what I was feeling, and I just wanted extra compassion and sympathy that night. Harboring these thoughts, I made my way out of bed and to the bathroom. Then the tears fell. Oh, how I had been a fool. Not only had my mom made my bath, but she had included a simple bath pillow. Her simple act of grace and mercy in the face of my bad attitude changed everything.

2. Prayer! This one is so, so important. It's always important to pray in any situation or relationship, of course, but this one is especially important. Don't forget that things are hard for them too. *Really* hard. And many people are going to be praying for you—not them. Pray for them, that they may have patience and strength. Pray that they may be renewed and refreshed, and that they may have rest. Pray that you would be able to show them love and that you would be a good patient.

3. Thank them. Thank them for everything, constantly. Being a caregiver is often a thankless job. Instead, we often do the opposite of thanking them, right? So, thank them. Sincerely. Frequently. From your heart. Even for the little things. I cannot emphasize this enough. And if words become meaningless (which they aren't), thank them through your actions and your attitude. Take the time to scrawl a note for them to find. Meet their eyes and smile. Give them a hug.

4. Resolve arguments, disagreements, misunderstandings, etc., quickly.

"In your anger do not sin": Do not let the sun go down while you are still angry . . .
(Ephesians 4:26)

This is simply wisdom. If things aren't resolved quickly, they will only get worse. And when the two of you are forced to weather unpleasant situations day after day together, trust me, you want to be on the same team.

You both already have enough battles. You don't need to be at odds with each other too. I can just picture a stony silence as a patient is too upset with their caretaker to ask them to help, say, tie their shoes and so simply leaves them untied resulting in . . . Well, don't you think it's just better to clear things up?

5. Submit to your caretaker's care. I know, I know, this seems a bit obvious, but it is so often easy to overlook. When your caretaker gives you a supplement to take—take it! When your caretaker asks you to do your doctor-prescribed walk (guilty as charged)—do it! It may not be pleasant, but don't take that out on your caretaker. They only ask us to do those things because they love us and want us to get better.

I could go on, but I think you're getting the picture. Loving the other person enough to try and make things easier for them, to forgive them, and to have mercy on them is the goal.

Relationships with the Chronic Illness Community: Don't Compare

I used to take health for granted. I assumed that most people were relatively healthy aside from the occasional cold and such. But when I got sick with a long-term illness, I realized my first mistake: taking health for granted.

At that point, though, I still thought that I was relatively alone as someone who was chronically ill. I mean, I knew other people were out there; they just didn't seem to be in the majority. And somehow, I never seemed to come across them. But of course, why would you expect to come across people with a long-term illness when you are only looking in places where healthy people generally hang out? There are plenty of Facebook groups, forums, websites, etc., for Christians with chronic illness. You just have to look.

And so, eventually, I realized my other mistake: thinking that I was relatively alone as someone with a long-term illness. Maybe reading this book is opening your eyes to that wonderful truth as well: you aren't alone! Or maybe, like me, by now you've come across so many people who, like you, are suffering from a sickness that it overwhelms you.

So much of our relationship struggles with other people in illness is in trying to communicate, longing for someone to understand, trying to sort through how different our lives are from most people around us. But one group of people poses an entirely different set of problems: those who are chronically ill. The ones who *are* in the same boat.

The chronic illness community is a precious and unique group. It's a group of people who daily live the things that we don't think anyone else could comprehend. From personal experience, they can relate and comfort and sympathize.

The thing is, like all human relationships, this doesn't come without struggles. And one of the biggest struggles I've noticed that many of us have within the chronic illness community is that of comparison.

The comparison trap is a nasty one. We think that we've defeated or ignored it only to look up and see the next person who is handling things better than we are. It comes in all sorts of shapes and forms and tries to sneak in when we aren't looking. It's exhausting and discouraging. Ugh.

Have you ever been trapped by comparison? I know I have.

See, here's the thing: we get sick. Then we want to try and figure out how to survive this sickness in the best way possible. So we look at how other people are doing it. And then we think, "Aw, they are doing this and that, I'm fine. They are handling things worse than I am, so I must be all right." We let ourselves off easy.

On the other hand, we might think, "They are doing things so much better than I am! Here I am, falling apart, but they are handling their mountain like it's a picnic! Where is their messiness? It must not exist."

Neither of these things are healthy or helpful for either ourselves or others. And the comparison is definitely not *fair*. For anyone.

You see, no one can see the whole picture. Likely, the person you are comparing yourself with has battles you can't even see. Ones you never will see or know about. When we think that someone is handling things worse than us, we are judging them . . . and only God is meant to be the judge. We are forming an opinion without knowing all the details. Perhaps someone could be trying harder or doing better. But that isn't our responsibility. Our responsibility is to do the best we can.

"Comparing ourselves to each other is like asking God who's the greatest in heaven all over again." -Bob Goff

In addition, when we compare ourselves to someone and think that they are doing so much better than we are—that we must be a failure —likely they have messes and struggles that we have no idea about. Again, forming a picture without seeing or understanding all the details. Tsk, tsk.

Besides all that, each and every person is different. Even if they are facing the exact same circumstantial battles—highly unlikely—each person has different strengths, weaknesses, support systems, pasts, etc. Comparison just isn't fair. Each person's battle is different no matter how similar they seem.

You know what? I've even tried to compare myself to healthy people! Just this morning, I was wrestling with jealousy and feelings of failure because I was trying to compare myself to my healthy brother. We're just so different, not only in health but also in our personalities, plans, and goals . . . that isn't a fair comparison!

Take it from me: don't compare yourself to other people. Just don't. There's only one Person you should be comparing yourself to, and that is God.

But just as he who called you is holy, so be holy in all you do; for it is written: "Be holy, because I am holy." Since you call on a Father who judges each person's work impartially, live out your time as foreigners here in reverent fear.
(1 Peter 1:15–17)

My dad used to have us do this object lesson when he would teach us about holiness. He would go to Home Depot and grab about thirty to fifty paint chips ranging all shades of white, black, cream, and gray. *All* shades. And then he would have us line them up in order from the purest white we could find (representing holiness) to the darkest black.

Let me tell you, that was incredibly difficult to do. Because, tell me, is slightly pinkish cream, slightly yellowish cream, or faintly bluish cream whiter? You can pick one that looks like really clean white, but likely once you put it next to a different white one, you will realize that it actually looks like very dirty gray.

The point being that other humans can look holy. But only one paint chip is whiter than all the others. God's standard of holiness is the one that we should reach for. We are to be holy not because other people are holy, but we are to be holy *as God is holy.* And in view of God's holiness and perfectness, we all fall short.

For all have sinned and fall short of the glory of God . . .
(Romans 3:23)

So then, is there hope? Yes. This is why we shouldn't compare ourselves to others. First, because their holiness is not what we want to go for . . . it's not enough. We are not better than other people. And second, because we need Jesus' blood to cover us because we can't get there on our own. We are not worse than other people or without hope of handling things in a God-honoring way. Just look at the next verse in that passage:

For all have sinned and fall short of the glory of God, and all are justified freely by his grace through the redemption that came by Christ Jesus. (Romans 3:23–24)

Instead of comparing ourselves to other people, we should be offering them the compassion and comfort that we desire for ourselves. Do to others what you would have them do to you, right? (See Matthew 7:12.) Remember, that comfort can't come from yourself, but from God (see 2 Corinthians 1:3–4).

We are told to rejoice with those who rejoice and mourn with those who mourn . . . it doesn't say anything about whether or not we are happy or sad, or if our experience is harder or better than the other person's. In fact, that verse is followed in Romans 12 with "live in harmony with each other".

Relationships with Family in Chronic Illness Part 1: Siblings

I'm the oldest of three kids. My brother, Silas, is just over a year younger than me, and a lot of the time, we could be twins. My sister, Nina, is about four years younger than me. Both are some of my best friends and I wouldn't want it any other way.

But, the thing is, we *are* siblings. And we do get into disagreements, misunderstandings, and all the things that come with living in the same house with someone.

Though I'm the one that is sick, their lives have also been hugely affected by my illness. They, too, have had to leave friends and home. They have had to completely change their lifestyles. They can't have friends over because of my sensitivities to chemicals and mold. They have a hugely increased chore load not only from me not being able to do what I used to, but also because there are even more chores that illness has added.

You know what? My siblings have been troopers. They are awesome and amazing, and I love them so much. But . . . things aren't always easy. For them, or for me.

Often, though they aren't technically my caregivers, they can take on some of those roles. I realize that sibling relationships are different for every family, but I want to take a moment to share some keys that I have learned.

First is to try to understand what they are feeling and going through as well. They may not be the ones that are sick to the same degree you are (or they might be), but that doesn't mean things have been a picnic for them. What they have going on in their life matters just as much as the things in our lives do. This is easier said than done but try to be compassionate. Put yourself in their shoes. Realize that it's hard for them to watch you go through this. That they love you even if you don't feel like they do. You are family. You are an important person in their lives.

Many of the keys that we talked about concerning caregiver relationships apply here, too. Resolving conflicts quickly? Important. Thanking them frequently? Important.

Also, try not to lash out at them. So, your body hurts? That's not their fault. That doesn't mean you need to belittle their stomach-ache just because you've had worse. Don't take out your frustration with your illness on them. They seem like easy, innocent siphons for our irritations, but just don't. It's not fair, loving, or kind. Plus, you want to maintain good relations with them. They will always be your siblings, even if other people come and go.

Finally, try extra hard to maintain and grow your friendships with them. With extra obstacles, it will require extra effort. But it will be worth it. I confess I haven't figured it all out. Far from it. I've been nervous about writing this section for quite a while. But this is something that is worth the difficulties.

Be creative! Maybe you can't go to your brother's football game. Then make sure to ask him all about it afterward. Try to be involved in your siblings' lives as much as possible. You can't play that board game with them? Then ask if they want to watch a movie with you instead. You don't have the energy to help your sister make that batch of cookies? Then put your book or phone away and have someone bring a chair to the kitchen so you can at least hang out with her while she does it.

As I said, I'm the oldest sibling, and sometimes I struggle with feeling humiliated because of my illness. When my siblings surpass me in school or other aspects of life, I can tend to get jealous or feel less-than. But as we talked about earlier, the comparison isn't fair (or helpful for that matter).

Another thing I would suggest is to be open with your siblings about your illness. Sometimes, I've felt like I needed to "protect" them from seeing me at my worst and I've tried to act like I'm doing better than I am. But I think perhaps that wasn't the best option. I'm not saying you have to tell your siblings everything. But when they know what you are feeling and going through it helps them to be able to help and understand you.

Illness can draw families apart. But it also has the potential to draw them even closer together. There are certain things you can go through with a person that will build trust and friendship, unlike most other things. And trials are one of those things. Fighting trolls is another.

Relationships with Family in Chronic Illness Part 2: Parents

Let's follow one tough section with another, shall we? Like my siblings, I have been blessed with wonderful, supportive, and loving parents. I often wonder how I could ever parent myself if our positions were reversed. I have been continually amazed and deeply grateful for my parents' understanding and mercy for me with all my issues that are results of illness.

That doesn't mean there aren't—you guessed it—road bumps and miscommunications. (Noticing a theme yet?)

I'll say it again: communication is key. Let your parents know your struggles, talk to them, and ask advice.

Also, when you aren't quite sure what to do about a particular issue, go to the Bible. It has a lot to say about relationships with parents, especially Proverbs. Just because we are ill doesn't mean that we are exempt from honoring, respecting, and obeying them.

Relationship with God in Chronic Illness

Finally, let's talk about the most important relationship to maintain —anytime—but especially in the midst of chronic illness: the one with God.

Really, that's what this whole book is about: glorifying God and continuing to seek Him even when we're sick.

I've observed that when people get a chronic illness, one of two things happens. One, their trial brings them closer to God and makes them incredibly strong in their faith. Or two, they run from God.

If you're reading this book, I'm guessing that you desire to continue seeking God even in your sickness. Here are just a few things I've learned about continuing to grow in your relationship with God through trials.

Go to God with your bitterness, praise, anger, frustrations, and questions. Run to God. Like we talked about in chapter one, He can handle all of it. We are never too much for Him. *That* is the secret to having faith in sickness, to growing closer to God in our trials. It's to allow Him to come into them with us.

We've talked a bit about how brain fog and other mental battles can affect our interactions or relationships with other people, but does it affect our relationship or interactions with God? Clearly, it can . . . I mean, take Scripture memory for one. It can be difficult to memorize Scripture when you can't remember what you ate or did five minutes ago, can't it? Or what about simple Bible reading? When our focus span only lasts upwards of two sentences (if that long), it can feel like we're failing God because we can't focus! Even prayer can be difficult when you can't remember what to pray for, or what to say. So what do we do?

First, take a deep breath and realize that it's okay. God knows exactly where each of us is. He is full of grace and love. We just need to learn to have mercy on ourselves. In life, the humans around you have to have mercy on you, right? Well, guess what? God's mercy and grace are so much bigger than that! And even more than the humans around us, God understands each and every detail of your heart and mind intimately—even better than you do.

The Bible says that in our weakness, God's power is made perfect. That His grace is sufficient (2 Corinthians 12:9). That means it is also sufficient for our quiet times and biblical disciplines. His love for us doesn't depend on us. Romans 5:8–9 says:

But God demonstrates his own love for us in this: While we were still sinners, Christ died for us. Since we have now been justified by his blood, how much more shall we be saved from God's wrath through him!

Yes, it can be easy to feel like a failing Christian when you have brain fog or other sickness struggles, just like it's easy to feel like a failing family member or friend or fill-in-the-blank. But that isn't true. Yes, we should still strive to spend time with God, and to do our best in these areas. But as long as our heart is in the right place and we are trying our best, it's okay if we can't be *the* best Christian we think we should be in this area.

So what if you don't think your prayers make sense because of brain fog—that's okay! God loves you and understands you.

While we're on this topic, I think it's important to address something else I've found in my own life. It used to be that I had quiet time every single day as soon as I woke up. However, things changed (and kept changing) when I got sick. Often, my body needed more sleep, and I wasn't able to get up early enough to do it right then. Or maybe my brain functioned better at a different time of day. Or our schedule changed depending on where we were living. Which was okay. You don't have to do it at the exact "right" time. It's not about rules and a checklist. It's about a relationship with God.

Another thing to keep in mind is simply to keep this in prayer. Tell God your struggles and ask Him to help you. Oftentimes, when my brain is simply too confused to handle reading (or even doing) anything else, I've found that reading the Bible is sometimes easier. God isn't going to give you a trial that will *make* you sin. He will provide strength, a way out, and mercy (see 1 Corinthians 10:13).

However, I want to leave you with a few practical ideas to help make biblical disciplines easier. For Bible reading, you could read the same section several days in a row, write it down, or read shorter portions at a time. For prayer, remember that it isn't about lots of well-thought-out phrases, pious petitions, or eloquent words. It's just about talking to your King. Another idea is to write thoughts down (or type or dictate if you have joint pain) as you pray or read—it will help you remember both as you go and when you look back on it later.

In the same way, the Spirit helps us in our weakness. We do not know what we ought to pray for, but the Spirit himself intercedes for us through wordless groans. And he who searches our hearts knows the mind of the Spirit, because the Spirit intercedes for God's people in accordance with the will of God.
(Romans 8:26–27)

Take It Deeper

In this chapter, we talked about all sorts of relationships, like the ones with caretakers, siblings, and parents. Keeping healthy relationships with others can be hard when you're dealing with chronic illness. But as we've discussed, ultimately, your relationship with God is the lynch-pin that will hold all the rest together.

So how can you strengthen your relationship with God? Spend time with God. Share your heart with Him and let Him share His heart with you. He wants to help you have good relationships with those around you. He wants to make you, and those around you, more and more like Him. Pray and ask God to help you grow in your relationships with the people around you. Lay before Him your struggles, your weaknesses, and your strengths. Pray through all the difficult things about each of your relationships right now.

Then, take some time to brainstorm steps that you can take today—right now—to begin mending the broken relationships and strengthening the struggling ones. Resolve any arguments that are causing bitterness and choose to forgive.

6. Teenager, Child, or Adult?

I was fourteen when I got sick, and now I'm sixteen—still sick. Just the other day, I said that I enjoyed being fifteen. My mom looked at me quizzically and asked, "You did?" I corrected myself to say that it had been quite a strange year, but I enjoyed being that *age*.

Often adults seem to mourn the fact that I'm sick as a teenager. But . . . I don't really feel like I'm missing my best years. They are definitely not wasted. God has a purpose in giving you trials in your youth. We settled that back in chapter one, right?

My sister and I share a room, and some nights we giggle and talk in the dark . . . sometimes way past our bedtimes. (Shhh! Don't tell anyone.) One night as we were getting sleepier and sleepier, one of us asked the other which Disney princess we thought the other was most like. (I can't remember who . . . It was late. Cut me some slack!) My sister told me I was most like Rapunzel. Nice. *Tangled* was one of my favorite Disney movies, so that wasn't so bad. I asked her why, and her answer was . . . interesting.

"Well, you have long blond hair, you like to read, and you're stuck in your 'tower' (bed) so often," she explained. A few months later she drew me a picture of Rapunzel for my birthday and wrote a beautiful letter to me on the back.

Her comparison got me thinking. I don't know if you've seen it, but in the Disney version of Rapunzel, *Tangled* (2010), the movie opens with a song. That song is all about the tower-bound princess wondering when her life will begin. While she waits, she certainly

75

isn't sitting around doing nothing. She paints and reads and cleans and does all sorts of things. But to her, it all feels sort of wasted.

If you are a chronically ill teenager, does your life feel wasted? Do you feel like you're stuck in a detour, waiting for your *real* life to begin?

Sickness has "taken" two of my growing-up years so far. I have many emotions about that time, but was it really taken from me? When time passes, it cannot be regained. Right now, a lot of my time is spent in bed, stuck at home, or waiting at doctor's offices. Maybe it is for you too. On the one hand, it is okay to mourn the feeling of the loss of our childhood. But on the other, we need to stop holding out for when "real" life starts. Real life is *now*.

Don't get me wrong—it's totally okay and even very necessary to hold on to the hope of healing. But we need to remember that we do have life now, too. We don't want to fall into the trap of getting so caught up in the past or future that we forget to live now.

Especially in our teen years. They are precious and will never be regained. We should use them for God! Even if that means simply striving to glorify and please Him as we are in bed, stuck at home, or going to doctor's appointments.

Our sickness—or whatever trial you are going through—isn't a detour. It's part of God's perfectly orchestrated plan. It's not just about pushing through until we get to the smooth road again. This part of our journey is part of our road.

I get it. I want this part of the road to be over already. I just want to finally be okay. Simply okay. Don't you? But God has put me here. And He has put you exactly where you are.

Will we choose to try and glorify Him in this part of the process, submitting to Him, and allowing Him to shape us into diamonds? Or will we lose all of that by *only* having eyes for the next phase, season, or adventure of our lives?

Don't let anyone look down on you because you are young, but set an example for the believers in speech, in conduct, in love, in faith and in purity. (1 Timothy 4:12)

Is It Good to Be Sick When We're Young?

While adults mourn our "wasted" years of sickness, those our own age often don't seem to understand us, and admittedly I have few friends that are my age exactly. But that's okay. By giving us suffering in our youth, God has given us a special battle and task. He must think we're strong, and yet so often I feel weak. But God knows what He's doing. The Bible even says that it's good to bear burdens and trials when we're young, look:

It is good for a man to bear the yoke while he is young. (Lamentations 3:27)

So *why* is it good to bear the yoke in our youth? There are definitely many pros and cons to being sick when you're young rather than when you're older. For example, I've been told that since I'm young, I'll bounce back faster and easier. And as we're only teenagers, we don't have a family to care for, a career to maintain, or whatever else. (Of course, there's the problem of school, but . . .) Then sometimes I think I'd rather be sick when I'm older so that I'd have to deal with the repercussions for less time of my life. But who knows?

As you can tell from the title of this book, one huge reason that I think God gives us trials is to shape us into His image. To train us. Specifically, to train us for what He still has in store for us in the future. Of course, sometimes this training feels less like army training and more like SEAL training, but God knows what He is doing. Why should we wait to learn these lessons if He knows that we are ready for them now?

Just imagine what amazing things He will do through you in the future if He's already to this hardcore stage of the diamond shaping! Sometimes that thought scares me . . . If this is the training and preparation, what in the world will He have for my future? But He loves me. He is perfect. And His plans are still to prosper me, to give me a hope and a future.

"For I know the plans I have for you," declares the Lord, "plans to prosper you and not to harm you, plans to give you hope and a future." (Jeremiah 29:11)

Self-Conscious

When we're in the grocery store, people of all ages (although it does often seem to be kids) stare at the mask I have to wear. When we go to a potluck, people look curiously at the jar (and I mean *jar*) of supplements I have to take with food.

Teenagers are supposed to be the ones who are the most self-conscious people, concerned about their image and being cool and accepted, right? We're not supposed to be dealing with any topic or situation more serious than school in our lives right now, right? At least that's what our culture says.

I struggle with some of the same things. We're human after all! One of my symptoms includes my abdomen bloating hugely every time I eat and then going down between meals. For a couple months it was especially bad. For the most part, I was all right with it and didn't mind too much what people thought.

But I remember one evening in particular when we were about to leave the house to go hang out and have dinner with a few families. I looked in the bathroom mirror and a tear slipped out. "I just want to be pretty," I whispered.

Another time I was at the youth theatre practice. Most of the time we sat on these long black benches when we were waiting for our scene to come up, watching some of the other kids act, etc. I sat down to wait, but instead of sitting on a bench, I lowered myself gingerly to the floor. Some of the girls came up to me.

"You can sit up here if you want to," they said, gesturing to the benches.

"Thanks, but I'm all right," I said.

"Are you sure?" one of them asked. I nodded and began to try and explain my joint pain. One of the girls soon nodded.

"Oh yeah, I have something similar, called juvenile rheumatoid arthritis," she said.

I'm glad that the girls understood, but I had still found myself at a loss to try and explain myself to them. Not many of them had known I was sick at that point.

Have you had similar experiences? You find yourself in the middle of a group of healthy teenagers with few cares beyond homework and you wonder . . . well, you wonder so many things. You wonder how to explain yourself (see chapter four), if anyone will understand (see chapter ten), and what they will think (keep reading!).

Let's go back to the bloating struggles for a moment. Contentment with my physical appearance hadn't been a *particular* struggle of mine before that. But God knew what I would need then. Multiple friends separately told me that I was "beautiful" and "strong" . . . When I certainly didn't feel like either of those things. God knew that I needed to be reminded of the truth. Maybe you do too. Maybe like me you've briefly lost sight of it. Let me remind you!

God loves you.

He made you perfectly.

He made you beautiful.

You are made in God's image.

And that's what makes you beautiful.

The bloating (or whatever it is for you) does not change that. The bloating will stop. It's caused by the sickness, a fingerprint of the fall. It's not part of God's good design.

Shall what is formed say to the one who formed it, "You did not make me"? Can the pot say to the potter, "You know nothing"? (Isaiah 29:16b)

For you created my inmost being; you knit me together in my mother's womb. I praise you because I am fearfully and wonderfully made; your works are wonderful, I know that full well. My frame was not hidden from you when I was made in the secret place, when I was woven together in the depths of the earth. Your eyes saw my unformed body; all the days ordained for me were written in your book before one of them came to be. (Psalm 139:13–16)

The Lord will vindicate me; your love, Lord, endures forever—do not abandon the works of your hands. (Psalm 138:8)

So God created mankind in his own image, in the image of God he created them; male and female he created them. (Genesis 1:27)

Maybe you've heard this a million times in your life already, or maybe this is a new message. But . . .

"God made you special, and He loves you very much."
-Veggie Tales

It. Doesn't. Matter. What. People. Think! It doesn't! And not in the world's way of "be yourself" and "rebel." No, God's opinion matters so much more. And He is a God full of grace and mercy. If He put you in your sickness, then He isn't going to scoff at you for being sick, for having joint pain or a bloated stomach. The King of the universe looks at your heart, not your body.

But the Lord said to Samuel, "Do not consider his appearance or his height, for I have rejected him. The Lord does not look at the things people look at. People look at the outward appearance, but the Lord looks at the heart." (1 Samuel 16:7)

Your body will get through this! Do you know what is harder, though, and more important? Your heart. Will your heart get through this? Will it come out beautiful, praising God? Or will it come out bitter?

Instead of dwelling on what people think of your outward appearance, be concerned about your heart, the part that God is concerned with. Ultimately, what will matter?

Besides, you will acquire many traits because of your sickness, aside from your bloated stomach, that people will notice. You are more mature than most your age. You have to live with pain. You have to live with limitations. If someone doesn't think well of you because of your bloated stomach (or whatever it is for you), they are not going to be someone who will stick with you through the rest of it.

I Want to Be a Normal Teenager

I just want to be a normal teenager. I want to eat pizza, go shopping, wear normal (modest) clothes, and have a life outside of doctor's appointments. I want my biggest concern to be school.

Today as I write this, the emotions overwhelm me. Yesterday, I ranted to a friend about a T-shirt. It was petty and ridiculous, but as she told me, emotions attach themselves to different things, and it's okay to be sad.

But as I was thinking about it more today, I realized that while so many times I just want to be a normal teenager, I also don't want to lose the things that God is doing in my life. This book, for example. I would never have had this sort of ministry opportunity if it weren't for my physical trials. I wouldn't live where I live and know the people that I do. God has allowed my life to touch so many more people through this sickness than it would have otherwise, all for His glory.

I'm not saying that sickness is something we should celebrate, but think about that next time you feel the desperate longing to just be a normal kid. Get out a piece of paper and write down the list of all God is doing through your sickness and all the people He has touched through it. So often, we don't realize all the people that are watching us as we lay in our lonely beds and quiet rooms seemingly cut off from the world.

A Two-Year-Old

If we're honest, the idea that people are watching us in this helpless state is humiliating. Not to mention frustrating. Often, I feel like a teenage infant. Unable to do so much for myself, forced to rely on others. All the way down to toting around bags of supplements and clothes, keeping strange things related to health in my purse . . . unable to even have a purse, but needing an even bigger bag! (Sound like a diaper bag, anyone?) I even had this filtered water bottle for a bit that some little girls we knew called "Sara's Sippy" (they were so cute, it made me smile).

At one point I wasn't even able to tie my own shoes. We arrived at the park for a homeschool get-together, and I would hung and asked my mom to tie them for me because of my joint pain. Yep, humiliating.

Other times, my brain fog or other mental struggles are such that I can be treated like a two-year-old by my family. Gently, kindly, and meant in love. They're just trying to help me as I struggle. But it doesn't make it any easier. I often wish that I could be a normal teenager.

But then God taught me—and is still teaching me—how to surrender my pride. To humble myself. To let go of those things and to choose to honor Jesus with humility. To care about what He thinks of me rather than caring about what those around me think. I've found that it actually causes those around me to respect me more in the end anyway. It's just difficult because it goes against my human nature.

Forced to Be an "Adult"

Then there's another aspect to it all that's sort of the opposite.

When I first got sick, I had to learn to sit on the sidelines when my friends played active games that required working joints or to not stay very long at birthday parties when I needed the energy to function. Or—well, really when they acted like teenagers. I had to learn to stand (or sit) on the sidelines with the adults.

Mind you, I enjoy talking with adults and such, but sometimes you don't want to be the only kid watching the fun-looking game of Fastest Tagger in the West. You want to run, play, and share in the laughter and friendly competition. But you can't.

Not being able to be a teenager when you *are* a teenager can be pretty frustrating and humiliating, can't it? Especially at first. The key is pretty obvious if you think about it, but also pretty difficult to learn or put into action. So, what's the key?

The key: humility. We have to let go of our pride and entrust our dignity to God's hands.

And patience. Patience is good too.

Often, I feel simultaneously so far behind all of my peers and yet so far ahead. I can't drive yet, and it's been years since I did math or normal school. I had to give up on my CLEP tests. And yet, God is teaching me other life lessons that most people my age may never know. I know what suffering is. I know how doctors work. I know what arthritis feels like. Maybe we feel "forced to be an adult." But a benefit of that is more wisdom and experience.

Learning to Be a Teenager Again

Then there's the other side of it all: healing from chronic illness and learning what it means to be a kid or teenager again, after being an adult as well as a child or infant for so long.

A month or two ago, my family was out hiking, and snow lay on either side of the dirt road we were walking along. My two siblings ran out into a larger section where there were fewer trees, laughing as they dragged each other over the snow on a sled. I smiled at them and made handprints in the snow at my feet on the edge of the field, where I was standing next to my mom, who was also watching my siblings and taking pictures. She looked at me.

"You don't want to play in the snow?" she asked.

"I . . . I forgot I could," I replied.

I was so used to acting like an adult in these situations that I had honestly forgotten I was physically able to play too now that I was doing better. I had completely forgotten to miss that type of playing since it just wasn't something I could do for so long.

A few weeks later, I was at the park with my family, waiting for someone, and I sat on a swing while we waited.

Then it hit me.

I couldn't remember the last time I had been on a swing. (When I was on the swing and realized that, I made sure to go really high, and then jump of course.) The same thing happened at one point with a slide.

All this to say, don't forget to be a kid when you can, even if sometimes you don't feel like it or don't feel like one. Have fun. When the healing process comes, there's going to be a lot that you'll need to relearn, and being a kid is probably one of them. Enjoy it! It may feel strange at first, but you of all people know better than to waste your years as a kid.

Perhaps hearing about feeling better and the opportunity to be a kid again hurts. You read this section and your heart sank. I'm so sorry. I want to give you a big hug right now and tell you that you will be okay. We will talk about hope in the next chapter, but hold on to the promises in the following verses:

Praise the Lord, my soul; all my inmost being, praise his holy name. Praise the Lord, my soul, and forget not all his benefits—who forgives all your sins and heals all your diseases, who redeems your life from the pit and crowns you with love and compassion, who satisfies your desires with good things so that your youth is renewed like the eagle's. *(Psalm 103:1–5) (emphasis mine)*

Take It Deeper

- Having chronic illness in your teen years can be hard. Often, we are tempted to begrudge it. But as we've talked about, God is using it to make us more like Him.

- Pray and thank God for this part of the road. Remember, it's not just a detour, it's part of "real" life. The good, the bad, and the ugly: it's all part of the journey.

- Speaking of the "ugly" . . .The Bible actually has a lot to say about physical appearance. There are so many more verses than the ones written out in this chapter. (Those were only the tip of the iceberg.) Take some time and check out the following verses as well: 1 Peter 3:3–4, Proverbs 31:30, Isaiah 45:9, Jeremiah 18:6, and Romans 9:20–21.

- Lastly, read all of Psalm 103 and meditate on what it means for you. Then spend some time in prayer. Ask God how you can best be using this time to serve Him, and trust Him with the limited strength, ability, and energy you have. His grace is sufficient, even when you can't do much.

S.G. Willoughby

7. Hope and Disappointments

"Oh! I see! Please CRUSH my hopes . . . and replace them with yours. Your ways are so much more. So much better. So much higher."
-Sara's journal, May 24, 2016

For the first nine months or so of being sick, I would go to the doctor every eight weeks. (Oh, those were the days!) Every eight weeks, I would be given a new medicine, supplement, or treatment. "This month, I'll get better," I thought. "This time it will work. In just a few weeks, I'll be back to normal." But I wasn't. I didn't get better. Bubbling, building hope, and then crashing, tumbling disappointments as yet another appointment drew near, and nothing was better. If anything, it was worse. Over and over again. It was a never-ending cycle.

Or even worse, there *would* be an improvement. Look! Sure evidence that this time I *was* getting better! Right? Which only resulted in a confidence crash later as things got worse again. Have you been there? Are you there right now?

What about when it comes to explaining to other people, who love you and are praying for you, why one day you're insisting that you're almost better, and then next you are bed-bound?

Eventually, you become afraid to hope, even when you do get better. You just don't want to be disappointed again.

Hope deferred makes the heart sick, but a longing fulfilled is a tree of life. (Proverbs 13:12)

Hope. I don't know if this sounds strange, but I picture hope as this beautiful bluish-white jewel, peeking out from a rock. A star in a sky of black. Anyone will tell you that hope is crucial to suffering well. But when it comes down to it, it's actually quite the—er—*adventure* to navigate how it comes into play in our lives and in our trials.

Why Do We Hope?

In chapter one, we talked about *why* we have suffering and trials: sin. In this chapter, we're going to talk about why we have hope. It's easy to say that we need it when it's a vague sparkling idea, but what about when it comes down to the nitty-gritty details? That's when we actually need to have a solid foundation behind our hope—otherwise, it won't last.

So what is the foundation for our hope? Well, it all starts with what we talked about in chapter one about the reason for suffering: sin. It's a bit ironic, but hope starts with great hope*less*ness.

We have hope because Jesus has saved us from sin, the reason we have these trials in the first place. Jesus sacrificed Himself on the cross for us and was buried. But this is the hope: it didn't end there! Three days later He rose again, saving us from sin; and get this, after spending forty days on earth with the disciples teaching them and proving His resurrection, He went up to Heaven *to prepare a place for us.*

Just look at one of the many things the Bible says about this place:

"'He will wipe every tear from their eyes. There will be no more death' or mourning or crying or pain, for the old order of things has passed away." He who was seated on the throne said, "I am making everything new!" Then he said, "Write this down, for these words are trustworthy and true." (Revelation 21:4–5)

No more! No more death or mourning or crying or pain. As Christians we are promised eternity forever in Heaven with God, free from all the consequences of this fallen world we live in. He will make everything new, including our bodies—the Bible says that we will be given heavenly bodies.

Why do we hope? We hope because we have faith in Jesus' resurrection, the cross, and the promise of Heaven. We have hope because we know that pain, suffering, trials, and sickness will end. They will end. And when we look at our time of sickness here on earth, however long it is, we know that it will be so short in comparison to the vast, unending expanse of eternity.

Praise be to the God and Father of our Lord Jesus Christ! In his great mercy he has given us new birth into a living hope through the resurrection of Jesus Christ from the dead, and into an inheritance that can never perish, spoil or fade. This inheritance is kept in heaven for you . . .
(1 Peter 1:3–4)

But now he has reconciled you by Christ's physical body through death to present you holy in his sight, without blemish and free from accusation—if you continue in your faith, established and firm, and do not move from the hope held out in the gospel. *This is the gospel that you heard and that has been proclaimed to every creature under heaven, and of which I, Paul, have become a servant. (Colossians 1:22–23) (emphasis mine)*

My dad describes eternity like this: Picture Mount Everest. It's huge. Over 29,000 feet. I mean, really, stop and think about it. That's an amazing height! Now picture a silk handkerchief or feather. Imagine how long it would take to wear the mountain down to dust with your feather. Got that in your mind? Imagining how long that would take? All that time is no more than a blink in light of eternity.

We get to spend eternity in Heaven free from sickness, death, mourning, or pain. Just imagine! Your body and mind and *everything* in perfect health. Perfect health. No sickness.

That is our hope. Just look at what Paul says in Romans 8:18:

I consider that our present sufferings are not worth comparing with the glory that will be revealed in us.

When we see that verse it's easy to think, "Sure, that sounds great, but really?" Yes, really. Paul knew what suffering was. Probably far more than any of us do. Have you ever been stoned? Whipped? Shipwrecked? Probably not. But that's only the beginning of Paul's suffering.

Are they servants of Christ? (I am out of my mind to talk like this.) I am more. I have worked much harder, been in prison more frequently, been flogged more severely, and been exposed to death again and again. Five times I received from the Jews the forty lashes minus one. Three times I was beaten with rods, once I was pelted with stones, three times I was shipwrecked, I spent a night and a day in the open sea, I have been constantly on the move.

I have been in danger from rivers, in danger from bandits, in danger from my fellow Jews, in danger from Gentiles; in danger in the city, in danger in the country, in danger at sea; and in danger from false believers. I have labored and toiled and have often gone without sleep; I have known hunger and thirst and have often gone without food; I have been cold and naked. Besides everything else, I face daily the pressure of my concern for all the churches.
(2 Corinthians 11:23–28)

And yet he says that in light of Heaven our present sufferings are not even worth the comparison in the reality of the glory that will be revealed in us.

Do you remember how I named my blog R535? Well, the reason I named it that was because of Romans 5:3–5:

Not only so, but we also glory in our sufferings, because we know that suffering produces perseverance; perseverance, character; and character, hope. And hope does not put us to shame, because God's love has been poured out into our hearts through the Holy Spirit, who has been given to us.

Are you grasping the significance of that? Paul is saying that suffering produces many things, but in the end, it produces hope. Suffering seems like the sort of thing that would do the opposite; it seems like suffering would suck hope away. But it doesn't. According to this verse, it *produces* hope. Why? How? It forces us to rely on something other than ourselves. Things are hard, so we have to hold on to something better.

Hope Does Not Put Us to Shame

The last part of that passage has another very important point, though. *Hope does not put us to shame, because God's love has been poured out into our hearts through the Holy Spirit, who has been given to us.*

There are hopes that do put us to shame . . . but I think that's because they aren't *real* hopes at all. Hope isn't wishful thinking. It isn't luck. It isn't naïve. It isn't wimpy. Hope recognizes the pain and suffering all around us, but it trusts in God's love, promise, and incomparable power.

Hope does not put us to shame because of two things: God's love and the Holy Spirit. Ephesians chapter four talks about how we are marked with His Holy Spirit *for the day of redemption*. It is a seal, declaring our inheritance: eternity in Heaven.

The hope God has given us isn't something that will float away, but a gift we can possess and hold on to.

Let's look at that Romans 5 verse again. Because God's love *has been poured out into our hearts through the Holy Spirit, who has been given to us.* His love is poured out into our hearts. Through the Holy Spirit that has been given to us. Those are things that we can possess and hold on to.

Be strong and take heart, all you who hope in the Lord.
(Psalm 31:24)

Hope May Be Hard to See

"When a train goes through a tunnel and it gets dark, you don't throw away the ticket and jump off. You sit still and trust the engineer."
-Corrie ten Boom

Hope requires faith. Because you know what? It doesn't always make sense. Take Abraham, for example. God promised him that he would be the father of a nation . . . but here he was, a very old man with an elderly wife, and no glimpse of even one child. As we know, God fulfilled His promise perfectly. But Abraham didn't know that. In his eyes, there was no logical reason to hope. It seemed impossible that Sarah would bear him a child. It was simply *against all hope*. However, Romans 4:18 says,

Against all hope, *Abraham in hope believed and so became the father of many nations, just as it had been said to him, "So shall your offspring be." (Romans 4:18) (emphasis mine)*

Yes, hope requires faith. Hope is the light at the end of the tunnel. But sometimes the tunnel bends and we can't see it. The light may be right around the corner, and we just don't know it yet.

***

One time, my mom got lost. She'd gone out for a run and had no idea how to get back home. She tried to ask people for help but was hindered because at the time we were newly moved to South Korea, she didn't speak much Hangul, and she was finding it difficult to locate someone who spoke enough English to give her directions.

She asked person after person until finally, someone flagged down a policeman. Here she was, in her running clothes, in a foreign country, with no one she could really communicate with, in the back of a police car.

Wow.

But it gets even better. She turned out to be only about two blocks from the international school where she worked. She'd been wandering around for such a long time, unable to find her way there . . . but she was basically there anyway! The police dropped her off and drove away.

Talk about an adventure. That was only one of the other humorous adventures we had living in South Korea. But it got me thinking.

Is it possible we're in the same type of situation? We're in our darkest moment, and all hope seems lost. King Théoden dies, Aslan dies, the Resistance is thwarted, the aliens are pouring through the portal in the sky. We don't see an end, all we see is defeat. When you're the person watching the movie or reading the book, it doesn't seem that bad, because you know that all turns out well in the end: Éowyn defeats the Witch-king, Aslan roars, the Resistance continues, the portal is closed.

But in real life, when there's no end in sight, we want to give up. The thing is . . . the triumph might be right around the corner! We don't want to be the marathoner who quit with only one mile until the finish line. God will give you enough strength to get through it. Don't give up hope.

Victory may be right around the corner! When did Éowyn kill the Witch-king? Immediately after Théoden died and the battle was waged. When did Aslan rise from the dead and defeat the White Witch? After his horrible death, after Susan and Lucy's night of weeping, after so many were turned to stone. Only then did victory come.

Or for that matter think of Jesus. Dead, gruesomely killed on the cross. His disciples locked themselves in an upper room, terrified and heartbroken. Utterly defeated. But then Jesus was raised from the dead, then He spent forty days with them before returning to Heaven to prepare a place for us.

Think of David, unable to fight for his country, hearing of his best friend's death, after having spent years on the run. Surely he was tired, worn out, and deeply hurting. Yet that was when God raised him up to be king of Israel, allowing him to defeat his enemies and those who attacked his nation.

Think of Esther, an exile and orphan made to be one of the king's beautiful women in place of Vashti, and then finally made queen . . . a position I wonder if she even wanted. Imagine finding out that her entire people, including those she loved, were going to be slaughtered by permission of her very own husband, and then the faith, courage, and resignation it must have taken to face the king. But then God destroyed Israel's enemies and blessed them. All was well, and Esther was favored.

Maybe right now you feel like you simply can't hold on any longer. I know it's incredibly hard. And I may not even be able to fully understand your individual story and what you are going through. I'm sorry. But here's what I do know: God won't give you more than you can handle in Him. He will equip you to fight your battle and endure your trial.

Just hold on a little longer. You may have years to go in whatever you are facing, it's true. But you may also have only a little bit left. Don't give up. Finish strong. Keep on fighting! You can do it. We can do all things through Christ who strengthens us.

Not that I have already obtained all this, or have already arrived at my goal, but I press on to take hold of that for which Christ Jesus took hold of me. Brothers and sisters, I do not consider myself yet to have taken hold of it. But one thing I do: Forgetting what is behind and straining toward what is ahead, I press on toward the goal to win the prize for which God has called me heavenward in Christ Jesus. (Philippians 3:12–14)

The darkest times are the times when hope is the most important. Hold on to hope, hold on to Jesus, and keep going. Even though it's dark, don't forget to keep moving toward the light, toward the prize, toward hope (not away from it!).

For in this hope we were saved. But hope that is seen is no hope at all. Who hopes for what they already have? But if we hope for what we do not yet have, we wait for it patiently.
(Romans 8:24–25)

One thing that is wise to do is to move toward that hope *with people.* Not by yourself. That way when the tunnel has a bend, you can grab hands and be able to keep a hand on either wall, continuing to move forward. The dark is a lot less scary when someone else is with you.

When hope is hard to see (or even when you *can* see it), invite people in. Continue moving toward our hope—the hope of Heaven —together.

Let us hold unswervingly to the hope we profess, for he who promised is faithful. And let us consider how we may spur one another on toward love and good deeds . . . (Hebrews 10:23–24)

Hope is a choice. It's a battle. It doesn't come automatically preprogrammed into humans. But it is also a gift from God. Our hope comes from Him. Not from anything else: not from health, a diagnosis, a human, a new treatment—anything. Our hope comes from God. The One whose love for us surpasses anything. And since He loves us, since He sent Jesus as a sacrifice . . . we have hope. We have faith in His love, and in His love, we have hope.

Yes, my soul, find rest in God; my hope comes from him.
(Psalm 62:5)

The Lord delights in those who fear him, who put their hope in his unfailing love. (Psalm 147:11)

Why, my soul, are you downcast? Why so disturbed within me? Put your hope in God, for I will yet praise him, my Savior and my God. (Psalm 42:5)

Hope for Healing on Earth

So far, we've been talking about the hope of no sickness or suffering in Heaven. However, it's also important not to give up hope of healing here on earth either. Even if your condition seems hopeless or is pronounced incurable.

When I was four years old and we were living in South Korea, I got sick. Very sick. It turned out that I had pneumonia and pleurisy. The doctors didn't know if I would make it. They really didn't know.

My memories of that time are vague, more like snapshots of scenes . . . Nurses changing test tubes. My IV bag. Eating cereal with my dad and a family friend in a hospital bed. Driving around in a taxi with the school nurse, calling hospitals. Lying in my bed, listening to the fluid in my lungs as I breathed. X-rays. Drawing blood. Coloring with the nurses. The doctor.

I was in the hospital for nine days. It got to the point where I had so many pockets of fluid in my lungs that the doctors were not able to put in as many chest tubes as I needed. To determine which part needed it the most, they took an x-ray.

A few hours later, however, they still couldn't decide which part was the most important. Nothing had come out into my drainage bag from the other tubes, and people all around the world were praying for me.

So they took another x-ray. In broken English, the doctor told us that it was a miracle. There was no fluid left in my lungs. It was all gone, and they had no idea where. It was a miracle!

You guys, God *still* does miracles! I've seen them personally in my own life. Don't give up hope for healing here on earth! Trust in God's power to heal you miraculously or to use doctors and medicine to heal you if it is in His will.

It's twelve years later, and I've been praying for over two years that God would heal me, and He hasn't, even though He has done it before in my life. And yet, I trust in His power, and I continue to hope in His healing here on earth as well, whether it's miraculously or through human treatment. However, we'll get more into all things prayer and chronic illness in an upcoming chapter, so hold tight for now.

Please Crush My Hope

Hope is one of those lessons that every few months—give or take some—it seems I have to learn all over again. I suppose that makes sense when we think about the cycle I outlined at the beginning of this chapter: hope, disappointment, hope, disappointment. The thing about true hope, however, is that no matter how often it is tested, it endures. Even when it has been dashed over and over again.

And now these three remain: faith, hope and love. But the greatest of these is love.
(1 Corinthians 13:13)

Sometimes I wonder why God repeatedly continues to allow my hopes to be crushed. But I think that in reality, it isn't real hopes that He is crushing . . . just small, false hopes. Maybe my dreams aren't working out, but guess what?

God's dreams are. And His dreams for me are so much bigger than I could ever imagine. Maybe God is allowing your future dreams and hopes to be ripped away, but He's replacing them with a gift. He's not just allowing your dreams to be ripped away, instead He's refining them—if you will let Him.

I once drew a picture in my journal. Now, I'm not a very talented sketcher, so it wasn't amazing, but it was how I pictured my hope. I drew a diamond. But the diamond started out surrounded by rock, with just a bit of the gem peeking through. The diamond was moving in one direction, but soon it hit a wall. *Smash.* Rock flew everywhere. It kept moving, and *smash*, it hit another wall. And another. Slowly but surely all of the rock was getting torn off and left behind. In my mind, the diamond was hope, and the rock surrounding it was all of the false hopes and dreams that were hiding it from view . . . the walls were the trials. God was doing that to my hope . . . smashing it against the walls of trials. But it was a good thing, because it was slowly resulting in my finding the real, raw hope that was the beautiful diamond.

As for me, I will always have hope; I will praise you more and more. (Psalm 71:14)

Take It Deeper

As we've already talked about, hope can be a rather broad subject. The number of Bible verses about hope can be overwhelming. It was very difficult to limit the ones already in this chapter. However, that doesn't mean we shouldn't read them. Especially because hope is so important—and yet so hard—when it comes to chronic or long-term illnesses. There is so much we weren't able to talk about in this book, and so much I have still to learn.

So today, just look up the word "hope" in the back of your Bible, or on your Bible app and dive in. Romans 12:12 is a great verse to start with: *Be joyful in hope, patient in affliction, faithful in prayer.* Read it, meditate on it, and even memorize it! It's short but full of an incredible amount of truth and lessons.

Thinking about how our hope is in heaven, I'd also recommend reading Psalm 73. Everyone who suffers from illness needs to read that psalm. There is so much truth and encouragement in that one passage of Scripture.

Lastly, and most importantly, pray. Pray and ask God to replace your dreams with His. Pray and ask God to open your eyes to see things the way He does. Pray and ask God to fill you with true hope, His hope.

8. Resting in the Storm

"I'm tired. I'm tired of pain. I'm tired of not knowing. I'm tired of restlessness. I'm tired of irrationality. I'm tired of fighting. I'm tired of the battle. I'm tired of relying on others. I'm tired of being a burden. I'm tired of bed. I'm tired of being sick. I'm tired of being the 'sick girl'. I'm tired of being tired!!"
-Sara's journal, January, 2017

Rest. What a beautiful word. Don't you think? In chapter two, I told you about the survey I took asking people what one word they would use to describe chronic illness. If you remember, one of the ways most people described it was with words relating to change. Well, there was one other type of word used more often than the words relating to change to define chronic illness. They were words relating to tiredness, challenges, weariness, and . . . rest.

During a month or two when I was doing really badly, I didn't think that I needed any more rest. In my mind I was more picturing Edna from *The Incredibles* slapping me with a newspaper, telling me to pull myself together. "Get up! Fight!"

I felt guilty for spending all my time in bed doing nothing but resting. At least it *seemed* like that was all I was doing. In truth, I wasn't actually resting, despite all the time spent on my mattress staring at the ceiling.

You see, what I eventually learned is that resting is a whole lot more than just being physically still. Maybe it *looks* like you're resting, but that doesn't necessarily mean anything. For those with a chronic illness, even lying on the couch not moving often still means that you are fighting a battle. The battle doesn't let up, and it hasn't ended.

Around that time, a friend asked how I was doing and I said that I was tired. Yes, despite my belief that I was over-rested. I was tired of the constant battle of health, tired of the mental struggles I didn't know how to face, tired of having to rely on others, and tired of feeling like I was a burden to them.

I was tired of sickness, and, frankly, just plain tired of being tired. She told me that as she was praying for me, one word came to mind: rest. Just rest. You're allowed to rest. You need rest. Jesus says in Matthew 11:28–30:

"Come to me, all you who are weary and burdened, and I will give you rest. Take my yoke upon you and learn from me, for I am gentle and humble in heart, and you will find rest for your souls. For my yoke is easy and my burden is light."

There were two main things I was forgetting. We just talked about the first: rest is so much more than just lying in bed or on the couch. That is only one tiny form of rest. We also have to learn to rest and be refreshed mentally, spiritually, and emotionally.

One day, I was struggling. I wasn't doing well, and tears were just under the surface. Either we were headed out of the house, or people were coming over—I can't remember—but whatever the situation was, I did not have time to deal with my emotions. Instead, I was about to need *more* mental and emotional reserve to show God's love to and interact with the people I was soon to be surrounded by.

Checking the clock, I allowed myself five minutes. I slipped into my bedroom, closed the door, and took a deep breath. I couldn't allow myself to let the tears fall yet—that would have to wait until later. "God," I prayed, "I don't have the time or ability right now to deal with my emotions. Please refresh me mentally, emotionally, spiritually, and physically in Your strength, as I can't stop to rest at this moment."

And He did. His grace was sufficient for me, and He allowed me to get through the rest of that day even though I hadn't had the time to rest and recover myself like I needed. Which brings us to resting *in* the storm.

Resting in the Storm

The second thing I was forgetting was that it *is* possible to rest even when you're fighting a battle and life is going a thousand miles an hour. I know that sounds crazy, but it's possible, true, healthy, and necessary.

Even Jesus rested. When a storm was going on around Him, He rested both literally and metaphorically. In Matthew 8, we are told of how Jesus was actually sleeping in a boat smack-dab in the middle of a raging, billowing, tossing cauldron of a lake—a storm so fierce that even the experienced fishermen among His disciples were afraid they would sink! And that wasn't even the whole of it.

Jesus was in the midst of much more than just a literal storm. If you look at the rest of the story, you see that it was not only in the midst of a literal storm that Jesus rested but also in the middle of a lot going on in life around Him. He had just finished speaking with a crowd, healing many people, and now He was traveling in a boat to a place where He knew two demon-possessed men were waiting for His healing touch. And yet He rested.

I mean it. He was literally sleeping while the waves rocked the boat and the wind fought the sails. Resting in the storms.

Will we, too? Will we be like the disciples, stressed out, panicked, and terrified so much that they got rebuked for their lack of faith? Or will we, like Jesus, trust in God, come to Him, and allow Him to give us rest for our souls?

I challenge you: take a deep breath and cast yourself on Jesus. Pray. Be still and know that He is God. He is waiting with open arms. Choose to rest. If we take the time to stop and take our eyes off the storm, fixing them on Jesus, and realizing just how big and powerful

He is, all of the storms around us will seem small in comparison to His might and perfect plan. Just like Peter learned walking on water in the account of a different storm in the Gospels.

Survival Mode

For a few months during this sickness—er—*adventure* of ours, we were homeless. We had no idea where we would be living from week to week. God always provided a place for us to stay, be it a hotel, a friend's house, or our van. But it was a chaotic time.

My siblings and I joked that we had gotten packing down to a fine art. In thirty minutes the three of us, without any help from our parents, could have our entire "house" from clothes, bedding, and kitchen supplies packed up in our car without warning or explanation. Eventually, we would learn where we were going and why.

Talk about learning to adapt. We were in survival mode. That was definitely one of the times we needed rest the most but couldn't get it. Sleeping on air mattresses in a new place every night wasn't easy resting.

At that point in our lives, where we were living was also logistically and physically taxing. My mom had to carry the laundry a quarter of a mile every time she washed a load, and because we kept contaminating stuff, it had to be washed *a lot*. Apparently, wet laundry is heavy.

We were also working outdoors all day doing construction, cleaning dorms, or simply hiking back and forth across the beautiful camp property to do work or bring people lunch. We would collapse exhausted onto our air mattresses every day.

Survival mode. I'm sure you know exactly what I'm talking about whether it looks anything like the picture I just painted or not. Survival mode comes in all sorts of forms. It can come when life seems pretty normal on the outside, but inwardly it's a tidal wave.

I don't know how it looks outwardly for you, but survival mode isn't exactly the most fun place to be in, is it? Sure, it helps you get through, but wouldn't you rather thrive than survive? Especially once you've been in survival mode for months or years? It gets rather tiring after a while, doesn't it?

It does for me anyway. First, let's get something straight: survival mode is okay. Oftentimes, I think it is a gift to get us through hard times. It allows us to function without having to process everything in the moment. However, eventually, survival mode has to end. In something like a chronic illness that lasts years, it's important to learn how to thrive even in the midst of surviving—similar to resting in the midst of a storm.

Thriving isn't easy in difficult conditions. But the tree that grows even in the constant winds is stronger than the tree that grows in perfect conditions.

My family loves to hike. We have been blessed to see some pretty amazing places, but a few specific ones come to mind right now, especially the mountain heights where trees are sparse, or bluffs by the sea where the wind never stops whistling through the trees so much so that they grow leaning in one direction. But those trees are the ones I stop to admire, the ones I point out to my companions. The trees that grow in impossible places are so amazing because they have made it even in the trying conditions. They haven't given up. Even the ones leaning to the side, whose branches grew only in one direction because of the wind's constant influence, are amazing. Their twists and turns make them stand out all the more—in a good way.

You're allowed to be struggling. It's okay if things are hard. You don't have to always thrive. Survival mode is acceptable.

But you don't have to always be in survival mode either. We may be too weak, but in our weakness, God's power is made perfect. In Him, we can keep fighting and we can even go on the offensive. Don't give up trying to thrive even as you survive.

Longing for Vacation

I want a vacation. A vacation from my illness. There have been times where I thought I couldn't handle this for one more day; I just needed a break from sickness. Please? Just *one* day off?

Unfortunately, when you have a chronic illness, you can't take time off from it. Everyone else can, but not you. It is your constant, unwanted companion.

The end of your rope is a hard place to be. The light at the top seems so far away—too far away—and the darkness below seems never-ending. Our fingers are sweaty and slipping, and we don't know what's going to happen.

I often find, however, that those are the places where I seem to find God the most. Sometimes when things are hard, He seems distant. But other times, He scoops us up and carries us when we fall. When we reach the point where we desire a vacation but can't have one—when we reach the end of our rope—all we have to do is cast ourselves on Jesus.

It seems scary, letting go of our own hold on the rope when our strength inevitably gives out. But Jesus is faithful. When we let go of our own control, He can take over. And I don't know about you, but I think His hands are a whole lot more capable than mine.

Tired of Resting

But maybe you don't feel that way. Maybe instead of longing to learn how to rest, you feel quite rested, thank you very much. Maybe you feel like you have spent so much time resting that you never want to rest again. You are ready for life. You wish that you could be expending some energy rather than conserving it. Rather than resting. You're tired of resting.

Before I got sick we decided to make a garden. We did the math, measured the yard, and planned out eight raised garden beds. We ordered some supposedly good, fertile soil to be delivered, bought some shovels, and borrowed a neighbor's wheelbarrow so that we had two on hand. I'm pretty sure we even hired some of the neighbor boys to help. The morning arrived, and just like usual on an island near Seattle, Washington, it was raining. Our yard was mushy and damp. The dump truck appeared with the two thousand pounds of dirt that we had ordered.

We asked if they could back the truck into our yard and dump the dirt in or near the marked-off garden area. However, the moment the wheels hit the grass they began to sink. Well, that wasn't going to work. Instead, we laid out tarps and they dumped the soil right there in our yard on the edge of the road. We now had two thousand pounds of dirt to move about thirty yards to the garden and shape into raised beds within the chicken wire and material we'd already set up in the days before.

We spent the day shoveling.

Shoveling for that long is a fine art. Of course, I did take a few turns with the wheelbarrow, but you get the picture by now. It was a lot of work. But you know what? It felt *good*. It felt great to eat dinner that night and crawl into my bed (after a good shower). Sleep that you earned through hard work feels wonderful.

It was the same way with running before I got sick. Tiredness and rest that you fully need feels amazing. But now, those instances are few and far between. My body needs rest, but I feel guilty and frustrated that I didn't do anything to need it except function or stay alive.

Maybe you're feeling the same way—guilty and frustrated. First of all, don't feel guilty. Over and over again God has been teaching me that lesson: don't feel guilty for something you can't help or didn't do. Conviction is healthy and leads to repentance, but guilt for things that aren't our fault is unhealthy, and Satan wants us to be trapped in it.

Frustration on the other hand . . . that's a bit more difficult. I know it's hard, but we have to trust that God is in control and that He knows what He is doing. If He has chosen to teach us to rest by forcing us to do so, then maybe we should take the hint. Even if you've been resting for months or years—trust Him. I know it's hard, but if God still wants us to wait, then we should do our best to wait patiently. Patiently, and contentedly.

If you feel like you are over-rested and want something to do while you wait for your body to get the memo, then pray. This world always needs prayer. I'm sure it won't take you long to come up with a list that will take you hours to pray through. Read the Bible. Research theological truths in depth. Use this season to prepare. Be faithful with the things you *can* do while you wait.

I am so thankful for the times God has given me in my life to prepare for things I didn't know were coming. While I'm guessing that if you are reading this book you are in some type of storm— maybe you're sick or someone you love is sick—perhaps you aren't in any particular storm right now. Maybe there's a lull.

Don't waste that time! Use that time to rest, to recover, but also to prepare. It's the nature of storms to come again and again. Remember what we learned in chapter one: in this world, God has promised us trouble. Storms will come. But take heart! He has overcome the world.

Illness as an Excuse for Laziness

A friend once voiced something I've wondered too. She said, "The one question I consistently wrestle with is, 'Is all of the physical rest I'm taking *truly* required, or am I partly using my illness as an excuse to be lazy?' I don't want to expect too much from myself, but I also don't want to expect too little, and it's hard to find a balance sometimes."

As with many things, this is something that will be different for each person. I'm sure there are people out there using their sickness as an excuse not to do things at the expense of the people around them. If this is you, then I think I would do some serious thinking. God put you on this earth for a reason, and if He wants you to be doing something else, it might be wise to consider doing it. Just ask Jonah.

However, I would guess that the majority of people who have this question probably aren't using their sickness as an excuse to be lazy. Very few people wake up every single day with the goal of being lazy (unless they have a good reason, like a real need to rest). Being ill and fighting a physical and mental battle *isn't* laziness.

I get it. I'm frequently tempted from time to time to allow others to do things for me that in theory I technically could do. But on the other hand, it's good to be wise with the energy you have. If you can't do something, that's not being lazy. If doing something will make you feel sicker, it isn't laziness to let someone help you, even if technically you *could* do it.

When you can do something without major physical consequences, then do it. But we all know what it's like to flare, and most families would prefer you to not have to spend the next three weeks in bed and in pain just because you did the dishes one night.

You know yourself best, and if you are concerned, examine your heart. Ask God to help you to do the things you need to do, and to give you peace when you can't do other things. Ask Him to help you know when you are being lazy and when you truly aren't.

Actually, it's probably a good idea to examine your heart, actions, and abilities every so often just to be sure. Like I said, people don't usually wake up with the intention of being lazy, it just sort of seems to happen without us even realizing it. And illness is something that is constantly shifting.

Take It Deeper

- In this chapter, we discussed survival mode, resting in the middle of chaos, feeling *too* rested, and how resting is not only physical but also spiritual, emotional, and mental.

- So here's your assignment: Think through your life and

evaluate what areas you are lacking rest in. For example, maybe you need to give yourself permission for more sleep. Maybe you need to think about taking a nap. Maybe you need to make sure to have snacks at certain times for your mental energy (I know I do), maybe you need to set aside more specific times to meet with God in quiet time. I don't know—you do. But make sure you allow yourself to rest when you need it. It will help in getting better in the long run, you know. Don't feel guilty about it. A friend of mine knows this about herself— if she wakes up by herself in the mornings, not by alarm or anyone else, she feels so much better than if not. So she sleeps in late and works later into the night than I do, because that's how God made her body and mind to function best. And that's great! So what is it for you?

9. Peace in Storms

"I choose to let go of my anxiety and sadness and surrender them to You." -Sara's journal, March 13, 2017

Even more amazing than the truth that we can rest in storms is that we can have peace in them too. *Peace.* Another beautiful word. Peace isn't only outward but is primarily inward. Outwardly things can look calm while in the meantime there is inwardly no peace. And inwardly things can be peaceful while outwardly a battle is being waged. This is true in all areas of life.

Peace is a gift from God and a fruit of having His Holy Spirit in our hearts (Galatians 5:22). God's peace is something that we can't understand. Philippians 4:6–7 tells us how we can get peace:

Do not be anxious about anything, but in every situation, by prayer and petition, with thanksgiving, present your requests to God. And the peace of God, which transcends all understanding, will guard your hearts and your minds in Christ Jesus.

Pray. Surrender your fears to Him. It is so easy to be afraid. And with a chronic illness, there are so many things to worry about. Will we ever get better? Will we be sick forever? What about diagnosis? What will our future look like? Can we ever be a spouse or parent with this sickness? What if people get tired of taking care of us? What if we can't finish school? What if we run out of medication? What if we can't do what we want to when we grow up because of our sickness?

You know what? God knows the answer to each and every one of those questions. So, pray. Surrender it all to Him. Ask for His peace that transcends all understanding. Choose to trust Him, the King of the universe. Understand that His power is greater than anything you can face and that He is bigger than any mountain. He has given us the power that with faith as small as a mustard seed *we* can move those mountains. Fear God—not anything else.

But the Advocate, the Holy Spirit, whom the Father will send in my name, will teach you all things and will remind you of everything I have said to you. Peace I leave with you; my peace I give you. I do not give to you as the world gives. Do not let your hearts be troubled and do not be afraid. (John 14:26–27)

Peace in Anxiety?

I know it's *so* hard. Many of those with mental battles face crippling anxiety caused by the physical sickness going on in their body. How do you have peace in the face of that many-headed monster? It seems impossible. But with God all things are possible. That is the truth.

Anxious and irrational, I went through an immensely difficult two months. I remember the hours spent rocking back and forth, literally sobbing uncontrollably, pounding my fists into the floor. I remember my mom trying to coax me out of the closet. I remember my family laying hands on me as I shook, praying for healing and relief, for peace and calmness. I remember the irrational thoughts:

You're a burden.

They're upset with you.

You aren't worth it.

You're all alone.

You're sinning. Your faith is too weak.

You are nothing more than a broken, messy, sick girl.

You can't live up to what God asks of you.

Telling them would just add a burden to them.

They don't want to know.

I can't ask for prayers, I've already asked too much.

I don't know who I am anymore. I've lost myself.

This will never end.

Those lies hurt. I *knew* that they were irrational. I knew that they were lies . . . logically. But somehow, it was incredibly difficult to really believe. So how do we defeat the lies? How do we overcome the anxiety and have peace?

As with depression, we have to realize that a lot of this *is* caused by things in our body that we can't control and by physical things wrong in our brain. It isn't a sin that we have them.

However, God still has given us the power to have certain forms of self-control. And not all of it is our bodies. As a friend recently said, our enemy, Satan, often attacks us when we are at our lowest and our defenses aren't up. We are in a constant war. I know it's hard. I know. It seems like no one else understands, no one else can help us (more on that in the next chapter), but God knows.

No temptation has overtaken you except what is common to mankind. And God is faithful; he will not let you be tempted beyond what you can bear. But when you are tempted, he will also provide a way out so that you can endure it.
(1 Corinthians 10:13)

It's a fine balance between mercy and self-control. All God asks of us is our best. If you know in your heart that you are allowing sin in your life, then repent and choose to try harder. But if you know in your heart that you don't have any more to give, that you are doing your absolute best to please God, then don't get trapped by guilt.

One of my biggest concerns about anxiety is always that I'm sinning by struggling with it. It's true that the Bible frequently says not to be anxious, to have self-control, and not to fear. But it's also true that physical things happening in our mind and body aren't always under our control. It's not a sin to sneeze or to vomit. It isn't a sin to struggle with mental illness. However, it's not always black and white. A lot of the time the physical *is* mixed with the spiritual.

So, what do you do when you don't know if you are sinning or not? We'll discuss how to fight anxiety and irrationalness in a moment, but first we need to address when it's sin and when it's not. And that's not easy. I can't give you a checklist. I can't see your heart. And even if I could, I probably wouldn't know. After all, you see your own heart, and you probably are still confused and concerned, right?

But there is One who can both see your heart and understand it . . . and who definitely knows what is right and wrong. Yep, God. If you are worried that you might be sinning, here's what you do: ask God.

It's as simple and as difficult as that. He wants to help you. He wants to guide you. He desires you to glorify Him and do what is right. Just ask.

But who can discern their own errors? Forgive my hidden faults. Keep your servant also from willful sins; may they not rule over me. Then I will be blameless, innocent of great transgression. May these words of my mouth and this meditation of my heart be pleasing in your sight, Lord, my Rock and my Redeemer. (Psalm 19:12–14)

Remember also to check Scripture if you still aren't sure. Earlier in Psalm 19, it says:

The law of the Lord is perfect, refreshing the soul. The statutes of the Lord are trustworthy, making wise the simple. The precepts of the Lord are right, giving joy to the heart. The commands of the Lord are radiant, giving light to the eyes.
(Psalm 19:7–8)

Finally, ask other people you know and trust to help you work it out. So many of us, including myself, struggle to speak about anxiety. We are afraid of how people will react. But God didn't create us to try and go through life alone.

If you are wondering if something you are doing is wrong, ask a spiritual mentor what they think. Now, please be wise and careful with this. It can be very difficult for people to understand, and if they don't understand the medical side of things behind your mental illness struggles, they may be prone to say that all of it is a sin . . . which it isn't necessarily. And the same is true in reverse. Other people may not remember the spiritual side of things and may focus on the medical side. Remember, they are human. Be cautious in asking the specific question, "Am I sinning by struggling with this?" Be wise. But be willing to ask for and accept help. Ask someone who you know will be honest, who will listen to God's guidance, who will check Scripture, and who knows you well. Maybe even someone who has experienced something similar for themselves. It's a tall order, I know, and it will be different for each person, but invite people in.

Anxiety has been one of the biggest battles of all in my own personal war with sickness. I know how utterly helpless it makes us feel, how impossibly lost we seem. I so desperately wish that I could take that immense burden from you. Oh, how I want to make it better! But I can't.

We have to trust God and hold on to Him with all our might even if that's all we can do. If we have no strength left to move, and all we can do is look at Jesus as we lie there on the ground, then that's okay. That's okay.

Discerning the Lies

Okay, here we go. Let's talk about how to have peace in anxiety. First, however, we need to determine how to know if something we are thinking is a lie or not. Some are obvious. But others not so much, especially when we can't think clearly or calmly. We have tried to think through it ourselves, we have prayed about it, we have tried to think through Scripture . . . but that's just it: it requires thinking. Sometimes we need help. This is where people come in.

When you get to a point where you can no longer trust what you think or feel and you cannot trust your mind or emotions, ask for help. It's so hard because that's how you analyze everything in life . . . whether the pan on the stove would be hot to touch, or if that person across from you is upset or not. Every little thing.

How do we know which way is up or which way is down? What is right, and what is wrong? What's really going on around us?

Ask.

In *The Hunger Games*, ***spoiler*** Peeta gets tortured and his memories get twisted. Suddenly, he doesn't know what is right, or whom to believe. Should he believe those who say they used to be his friends? How can he know what is right when something different is coming at him from every direction?

Finnick gives him the same advice my mom gave me: "Just ask." Ask those around us that we know and trust. (I suppose that wouldn't quite work for Peeta since he didn't trust them, but at least when he asked he could have some information to try and determine the truth of).

Yes, others may not know exactly what is going on in our brains. But they love us. When we verbalize the things in our minds, they can help us determine if it's true and rational or not.

I know that it is often so much easier not to say anything out loud. Often, one of the irrational thoughts in my head is exactly that: that I can't say it aloud to anyone. But in doing that, I cut myself off from help, from understanding, and from compassion.

Peeta took to stating something in his head and asking, "Real or not real?" Why can't we do the same thing? If we ask it in that way, too, it can help our family or those around us realize why we're asking, so that they can help us.

So, ask, "Real or not real?" God doesn't mean for us to try and fight through everything on our own. He's given us Himself, His Word, and also the people around us.

Fighting with Truth

So, once we recognize the anxiety or lies, how do we have peace in it? In panic attacks? How do we deal with the irrational lies that scrape and scratch at our minds? To be honest with you, I don't have all the answers. But one way is to replace the lies with the truth. When we feel ourselves losing our sanity, we remind ourselves or ask others to remind us who we are, whom we belong to: God. We are His. We are princes and princesses. We cannot forget our identity.

Just as Jesus defeated Satan in the desert with God's Word, so we should speak His truth aloud. Hebrews 4:12 says:

For the word of God is alive and active. Sharper than any double-edged sword, it penetrates even to dividing soul and spirit, joints and marrow; it judges the thoughts and attitudes of the heart.

God's peace surpasses all understanding. I have prayed and prayed for His peace as I cried. Sometimes I felt it, other times I wondered where He was. But even in those times, when physically and mentally I was a mess, I often felt His whisper over and over again: "I love you. My child, I love you. Sara, I love you."

It's incredibly hard to pray when your mind is in rebellion against all sanity. Anxiety and panic are overwhelmingly loud, drowning out all else. But I learned that peace was more than physical or mental. God's peace was in my heart, even when I felt disconnected from it. The Bible says in multiple places that we are not to have anxiety. But how are we to do that? 1 Peter 5:7 says:

Cast all your anxiety on him because he cares for you.

Because He cares for you. Cast it on Him! He is so much bigger than your anxiety no matter how huge it seems. God is bigger. And even in the midst of your anxiety, He cares for you. He loves you. He loves me. More than we could *ever* comprehend or imagine. How do we overcome anxiety? Cast it on Him!

Do not be anxious about anything, but in every situation, by prayer and petition, with thanksgiving, present your requests to God. (Philippians 4:6)

Like the bleeding woman or the leprous men, we can give our ugliness to Him, and He is big enough and strong enough to handle it. We will never be too much for Him.

When I said, "My foot is slipping," your unfailing love, Lord, supported me. When anxiety was great within me, your consolation brought me joy. (Psalm 94:18–19)

As I wrestled through my own anxiety, this became the prayer I should have prayed more often:

Search me, God, and know my heart; test me and know my anxious thoughts. See if there is any offensive way in me, and lead me in the way everlasting. (Psalm 139:23–24)

Beg God to help you. He sees and knows all. Ask Him to lead you in the way everlasting when you aren't strong enough to do it. He is faithful. He is faithful to complete the good work He has begun in us (see Philippians 1:6). He will not abandon us or leave us on our own. He is our lighthouse. When the storm rages on, He will be faithful to guide us.

When my heart was grieved and my spirit embittered, I was senseless and ignorant; I was a brute beast before you. Yet I am always with you; you hold me by my right hand. You guide me with your counsel, and afterward you will take me into glory. Whom have I in heaven but you? And earth has nothing I desire besides you. My flesh and my heart may fail but God is the strength of my heart and my portion forever. (Psalm 73:21–26)

I once listened to a sermon by Brett Harris, and he pointed out that though the storm clouds gather in dark mountains and it is hard to see the sun—hard to see God—the clouds cannot touch the sun. The clouds are minuscule and pitiful in comparison with the burning ball of fire in the sky. The clouds can't blot out the sun! They have nothing over the sun. It's just our perspective that makes it seem so lost to us, so far away.

Storms come. It is their nature. They come over and over again as the water cycle continues. But you know what? Storms also dissipate. They leave. There is an end. They burn themselves out until there is no water left for even a wisp of a cloud. It's their nature.

I confess, I still wrestle with this. I haven't gotten it figured out. The best I can figure out for myself—and to share with you—is the truth that the Bible has to say about anxiety. I don't know exactly how to live it all out yet, but I do know that God's grace is sufficient for me. In my weakness, His power is made perfect (2 Corinthians 12:9). And the same is true in your life. We can't have peace in our own strength. But we can come out victorious in these battles through God's grace and through being clothed in His righteousness, not our own.

Therefore, since we have been justified through faith, we have peace with God through our Lord Jesus Christ, through whom we have gained access by faith into this grace in which we now stand. And we boast in the hope of the glory of God.
(Romans 5:1–2)

Take It Deeper

- In this chapter we talked about defeating lies with the truth—God's truth. So let's do that. Below, I've listed some of the lies I mentioned, accompanied by their truths. Read through the truths, say them out loud, and then continue the list with the lies that *you* are struggling with.

- **Lie:** I'm a burden.

- **Truth:** Carry each other's burdens, and in this way you will fulfill the law of Christ. (Galatians 6:2)

- **Lie:** I'm all alone.

- **Truth:** "Be strong and courageous. Do not be afraid or terrified because of them, for the Lord your God goes with you; he will never leave you nor forsake you." (Deuteronomy 31:6)

- **Lie:** I'm nothing but broken, messy, and sick.

- **Truth:** So in Christ Jesus you are all children of God through faith . . . (Galatians 3:26)

- **Lie:** I can't live up to what God has asked of me.

- **Truth:** But he said to me, "My grace is sufficient for you, for my power is made perfect in weakness." Therefore, I will boast all the more gladly about my weaknesses so that Christ's power may rest on me. (2 Corinthians 12:9)

- **Lie:** I can't.

- **Truth:** I can do all this through him who gives me strength. (Philippians 4:13)

- **Lie:** This sickness is my fault.

- **Truth:** For I know the plans I have for you," declares the Lord, "plans to prosper you and not to harm you, plans to give you hope and a future. (Jeremiah 29:11)

- **Lie:** This will never end.

- **Truth:** And I heard a loud voice from the throne saying, "Look! God's dwelling place is now among the people, and he will dwell with them. They will be his people, and God himself will be with them and be their God. 'He will wipe every tear from their eyes. There will be no more death' or mourning or crying or pain, for the old order of things has passed away." He who was seated on the throne said, "I am making everything new!" Then he said, "Write this down, for these words are trustworthy and true." (Revelation 21:3–5)

12. Just Keep Praying

"He commands us to pray—He will listen." -Sara's journal, March 12, 2017

To pray or not to pray, that is the question. Which may seem like a silly question to some. I know at one time I would never have thought of it. You're sick? Then of course you pray for healing! But . . . with chronic illness, I've learned that it's not so simple.

Praying means to hope, and as we discussed in the previous chapter, hoping isn't easy. Sometimes, it feels easier to accept that we're sick rather than continue asking God to heal us. It gets tiring after a while, after all.

Wait a second. It gets tiring to ask for healing? Alrighty, then. I would think that asking for healing day after day is a lot better than giving up. Besides, it's not very difficult. However, it still is wearing emotionally to keep hoping. Hoping is a battle. It's only in Jesus that our hope endures. Often, we've given up praying without even realizing it. It just slowly faded into the background. Other times, we make a conscious choice to give up hope, to give up praying for healing.

"You are never without hope because you are never without prayer."
-Max Lucado

Another reason we ask this question is that, besides finding it emotionally easier to accept being sick, we begin to wonder if it is God's will for us to be sick. When we think through all of the things that God is doing in our illness, we wonder if we should even be asking for healing. Is it selfish? Is it not accepting God's will for our lives to ask for something different—to ask for healing?

I don't think so. Contentedness where God has put us is vitally important in all areas of our lives. But so is hope. Guess what? These things can coexist. No, it isn't wrong to pray for healing. In fact, we are told in the Bible to pray continually. When David and Bathsheba's baby was sick, David did not stop fasting and praying even though God had told him through the prophet Nathan that the baby would die. This was the man after God's own heart! He didn't give up. He continued to plead with God.

Abraham did the same thing with Sodom and Gomorrah. He pleaded with God repeatedly to spare the city for the sake of fifty righteous people. And then forty. All the way down to ten:

Then he said, "May the Lord not be angry, but let me speak just once more. What if only ten can be found there?" He answered, "For the sake of ten, I will not destroy it." When the Lord had finished speaking with Abraham, he left, and Abraham returned home. (Genesis 18:32–33)

Or what about Hezekiah, king of Judah? God sent the prophet Isaiah specifically to tell him that the illness Hezekiah suffered from was going to kill him and that he should put his affairs in order. But when Hezekiah prayed and wept, God relented and added fifteen years to his life. Not only that, but God also promised to deliver and defend Hezekiah and the entire city from the king of Assyria.

It doesn't end there. God also gave Hezekiah a miraculous sign and even told Isaiah exactly what treatment Hezekiah needed (see Isaiah 38). Prayer is powerful and important, people! God desires to give us power and strengths we'd never know or imagine . . . we just have to ask. I know you've heard this so many times, but prayer is certainly *not* to be a last resort. It is the front lines of the biggest battle. Every single step of the way, we should be praying. Boldly, as these biblical people did. James 5:16 says:

Therefore confess your sins to each other and pray for each other so that you may be healed. The prayer of a righteous person is powerful and effective.

We should not be shy in praying for healing. However, even after David's seven days of unceasing intercession for his son, he accepted God's will. He had been praying so hard that his advisors and officials were afraid to tell him that the baby was dead! But when David found out, he surprised them:

Then David got up from the ground. After he had washed, put on lotions and changed his clothes, he went into the house of the Lord and worshiped. Then he went to his own house, and at his request they served him food, and he ate. His attendants asked him, "Why are you acting this way? While the child was alive, you fasted and wept, but now that the child is dead, you get up and eat!" He answered, "While the child was still alive, I fasted and wept. I thought, 'Who knows? The Lord may be gracious to me and let the child live.' But now that he is dead, why should I go on fasting? Can I bring him back again? I will go to him, but he will not return to me." (2 Samuel 12:20–23)

Paul also prays repeatedly that the thorn in his side would be removed in 2 Corinthians 12. He says that he prayed three times, but then the Lord finally said no, and Paul accepted it.

Jesus Himself asked for another way out from the cross. He too prayed three times, surrendering everything to God's will each time.

He withdrew about a stone's throw beyond them, knelt down and prayed, "Father, if you are willing, take this cup from me; yet not my will, but yours be done." An angel from heaven appeared to him and strengthened him. (Luke 22:41–43)

When you pray, ask for God's will to be done. Don't be afraid to ask Him for healing. Don't give up praying. Through Jesus, the veil has been torn. We are able to have boldness before the King of the universe. But at the same time, surrender yourself, your life, and your health to Him. Choose to accept what His will is.

"If Jesus heals you instantly, praise Him. If you are still waiting for healing, trust Him. Your suffering is your sermon."
-*Max Lucado*, Before Amen

Pouring Out Our Hearts before God

In chapter one, we talked about bringing our questions to God. I told you how much of this book was born from my own personal wrestling before Him. I think that this is a struggle for many people: pouring out our hearts before God. People either think of God as a wishy-washy indulgent grandfather and therefore do not respect Him; or they think of Him as a brimstone and fire, judgment and punishment God who is watching our every move, just waiting for us to make one mistake. So they do not bring their hearts before Him. He is neither. Our God is a God both of unfailing love and undeserved mercy, and also of perfect justice. If we think of Him as only one or the other, we are missing the biggest thing God desires with us: a relationship. He created us to delight in Him and bring Him delight.

He created us, and then died for us, and He wants us to give our hearts back to Him. More than anyone else, God is good at listening. Let's go back to David after his sin was found out. As we know, he prayed and fasted for seven days. Psalm 51 gives us a glimpse into what some of his heart's cries looked like during that time. One verse in particular stands out to me as I read it with the topic of prayer in mind:

My sacrifice, O God, is a broken spirit; a broken and contrite heart you, God, will not despise. (Psalm 51:17)

God desires us to pour our hearts out to Him in prayer. Both the beautiful parts and the ugly parts. The strong parts and the broken parts. He wants our whole heart.

Trust in him at all times, you people; pour out your hearts to him, for God is our refuge.
(Psalm 62:8)

All of Psalms is a good example of this. Some people struggle with Psalms, wondering how the writers can go from one mood to another so quickly. One chapter they're celebrating victory and praising God's goodness, and the next they're angry with God and not afraid to tell Him so. But we could learn from them.

When we come to God, it should be in the fear of the Lord. After all, we are kneeling before the King of Kings, the Maker of the universe! The One who has power over all things. But because of what Jesus has done for us, we can also have confidence before God.

In [Jesus] and through faith in him we may approach God with freedom and confidence. (Ephesians 3:12)

Asking Others for Prayer

Asking other people for prayer can be hard on many levels. First of all, it requires us to admit that we can't do it. It requires us to confess that we are struggling, that we need help, and that we're not strong enough. It means overcoming our pride.

Yikes!

I once listened to a sermon by missionary Otto Koning, and he made a very good point. He said to not say "I'm fine" when you aren't— by doing so, we cut ourselves off from the prayer of our fellow believers. It's so much better to swallow our pride, humble ourselves, and ask for prayer! Isolating ourselves isn't helping anyone.

Yet again, God did *not* create us to fight trials alone. Prayer is one very crucial way to have help. Asking people to pray is letting them help as well as asking God for help all at the same time. Prayer is one of the most valuable weapons we have in this fight with chronic illness—really, in everything we fight in life. We don't want to miss using it.

Even harder than that for me, though, has been this: I don't want to ask for prayer because I've already asked for so much prayer. I want to send out an email to report healing, not to report another twist or turn in my health, another slip downhill. I don't want to share my burdens, I want to share something to encourage people. Sometimes, I even feel guilty for asking for prayer *again*.

How wrong this is! Trust me, that guilt doesn't come from God. That comes from the devil. He doesn't want us to ask for prayer, because prayer is mighty and effective, a formidable foe in battle against him. He doesn't want us to have God's peace or strength, he doesn't want us to be renewed with God's power. He wants us to lose hope, to fall into despair, to give up fighting and praying.

However, over and over again we are told to pray and to pray without ceasing. Even if God doesn't answer right away, we are told to pray. We were not created to be alone. We *need* the body of Christ to come alongside us and fight with us.

One friend expressed once that she didn't feel like asking for prayer because she was pretty sure no one was actually praying for her even when they said they were. "What's the point of asking," she wondered, "when they're just going to pat me on the back and say they're praying? . . . I know they aren't really doing it." Have you ever felt this way?

Ouch. I've been on both sides of it. I think that the best thing to do is to ask anyway. If you know someone doesn't really care, then it's okay not to share your biggest hurts with them. But really, it's their problem. Forgive them and move on. Ask God to provide prayer warriors for you who *will* pray. They can make all the difference.

Some days, I will be struggling, and even without me asking them to, I know that people are praying for me. Later that day or the next I will frequently get a message or email from someone I would never have expected letting me know they were praying for me. I smile and realize that I knew they were . . . I could feel the difference. However, this doesn't mean that we don't need to *ask* for prayer. We still do! After all, they're human. Sometimes God will just prompt them to pray at the right time. So if people aren't actually praying, learn from that, and be faithful to pray yourself when you say you will. A good idea would be to pray immediately . . . that way you don't forget.

Will Anyone Understand?

Another reason that we hesitate to share our struggles is because we are afraid no one will understand. We feel all alone. No one could possibly understand what it's like to have constant physical pain. No one could understand what it's like to lose everything you own because of mold. No one could understand what it's like to be the reason that your family had to move from a place they loved to the desert. No one could understand the guilt we feel when we're the reason our family can't go to church or bring their Christmas presents inside the house. No one could possibly comprehend what it's like to war with your own mind, unable to trust what you think or feel, not knowing what is right or wrong, which way is up or down.

No one will ever understand what it feels like to be a chronically ill teenager.

And you're right. Every single person is different, and everyone experiences pain in different ways . . . even if the physical parts of it are exactly the same (which they never are).

What a lonely life we are subject to! But y'all? While it is true that only God will ever understand us perfectly and completely, God does give people the ability to understand whether they've been there, done that or not. He gifts certain people with discernment and compassion completely beyond our human capabilities. I know this because He has blessed me with people like that in my own life.

Praise be to the God and Father of our Lord Jesus Christ, the Father of compassion and the God of all comfort, who comforts us in all our troubles, so that we can comfort those in any trouble with the comfort we ourselves receive from God. (2 Corinthians 1:3–4)

Any trouble! Not just those who have the same troubles we have. Which means that even healthy people can understand us, can have God's compassion for us, can be there for us.

In addition to that, while you may be surrounded by those who really do have no clue, you're not alone as a chronically ill teenager. You may have yet to meet any, but I can assure you that there are more of you, of us.

I used to think that I was the only one, too. But while I used to take health for granted, as I have been sick, God has continued to open my eyes more and more to see the incredible amount of people around me who are also suffering. You'd be surprised at how many chronically ill teenage Christians I have met. You are *not* alone.

Resist [Satan], standing firm in the faith, because you know that the family of believers throughout the world is undergoing the same kind of sufferings. (1 Peter 5:9)

Note for those who are not sick themselves:

Hi there. So, I know that in this section I talked about how we who are sick need to understand that you can understand us. That we aren't alone. However, let me warn you: that is the last thing you should say. Whether you understand or not is beside the point. Unfortunately, we won't think that you understand if you say that you do. If you say that you know you can't understand what we're feeling or going through, however, it helps us see that you grasp the magnitude of the battles in front of us. I know, I know, it's quite a paradox. I've learned from my own experiences, and I don't say "I understand" to anyone anymore. Even to those who are literally going through the same physical things I am, I rarely ever say it. Just a tip.

Praying for Others in Addition to Ourselves

When friends share their struggles with me a lot of the time, they share them cautiously. They don't want it to be too much. They don't

126

want to burden me with their struggles when I have many of my own.

Maybe you have experienced this yourself. People know you are sick, and so hesitate to share their own trials and prayer requests, thinking that they need to be there for you only rather than put any of their own burdens on you.

When I see people doing this in my own life, I smile and assure them that it is indeed the opposite. While I am thankful for their sensitivity, and sometimes I just can't handle one more thing, a lot of the time I have found that it is good for me to be there for them, even (and sometimes especially) when I myself am struggling. In fact, while I wish everything was okay for others, I appreciate being able to get my eyes off myself and my own suffering and help someone else, even if all I can do is listen.

I think it is one of the best cures for self-pity—it gives us perspective and opposes self-centeredness.

Praying for other people is important for any Christian, but I think especially for those who are sick themselves. When we can't do anything else, we can pray. When we are stuck in bed for endless hours staring at the ceiling, we can pray. When we can't communicate with anyone else, God can see through our brain fog. As our own sickness equips us to understand the suffering of those around us more, we can pray.

As you have probably learned in having others pray for you in your trials, don't forget to let them know that you are praying for them from time to time. You probably know how much it means to know that you aren't fighting alone.

A friend of mine once shared with me her struggle to pray for herself. I listened but wondered, "I don't have that same struggle. In fact, I pray for myself constantly. Is that wrong?" My friend said that maybe it was because I was the one who was sick. For her at the time, she had instead been the one called to watch those she loved fight through sickness. She had plenty of practice praying for others but wasn't as comfortable praying for herself.

I wonder if that is a struggle other chronically ill people have. We pray more for ourselves than for others . . . the opposite struggle than that of some of those around us (like my friend).

Don't get me wrong, though! Praying for ourselves is vitally important. We need to take God's truths and declare them for ourselves in Jesus' name. We need to pour out our hearts to Him as we talked about earlier. We need to acknowledge before Him our weakness and beg for His help. We need to keep hoping. We need to keep praying.

Take It Deeper

- Even though we just spent a whole chapter talking about it, I cannot emphasize enough the power that we have in prayer. There are so many books and sermons on prayer, and I didn't even attempt to talk about the most important aspects of it in this chapter (or book). My goal was just to apply it to illness. However, I'd definitely suggest you look further into it yourself!

- Start right in the Bible . . . check out Elijah's story, for example. Here are some references to start with: 1 Kings 17:1, James 5:17–18, 1 Kings 18:36–39.

- What better way to apply a chapter about prayer than to pray? Stop right now, take a moment, and pray. Pray with all your heart and faith for healing. And don't stop asking, no matter how long you are sick. Pray for the people you know. Start with your family and close friends and work your way out. Pray and tell God everything in your heart . . . the good, the bad, the messy, the frustrating, and the petty.

- Remember, you're not alone. Sometimes it's hard to pray yourself, and you just need someone else to be praying on your behalf. It's always a good idea to ask other believers to pray with you and for you; after all, that's what community is for: to stand with you, pray with you and encourage you. Ask someone you know to pray for you right now. Just start with one person. Ask them to pray for healing, or for strength, or for courage, or for peace . . . whatever you need right now.

S.G. Willoughby

11. Moving Mountains

"Sarah laughed at Your promises. I pray that I'm not guilty of the same thing." -Sara's journal, December 15, 2017

Looming, huge, ginormous. The mountains rise in front of you. And not only in front of you but all around you. Layers and layers of them. Though it seems impossible, if you were able to make it past the first one, there's no way you could make it past the layers behind it.

They are mountains of questions, of school, of sickness, and of the future. Maybe literal mountains, even. You can't see beyond them and you have no idea how you're going to get over them. You don't know how to climb, and you can't catapult yourself over them—you'd just go splat.

What to do, what to do?

First of all, we have to realize that as big and huge and overshadowing as the mountains are, God is bigger. So much bigger. In this chapter, we're going to be talking about what it means to trust God and to have faith even in the midst of the mountains and trials that face us.

Guess what? God has given us the ability to move those mountains. Imagine that! A friend of mine recently wrote a great article about that very topic. Just look at the verse below:

He replied, "Because you have so little faith. Truly I tell you, if you have faith as small as a mustard seed, you can say to this mountain,

131

'Move from here to there,' and it will move. Nothing will be impossible for you." (Matthew 17:20)

Matthew 21:21 also says:

Jesus replied, "Truly I tell you, if you have faith and do not doubt, not only can you do what was done to the fig tree, but also you can say to this mountain, 'Go, throw yourself into the sea,' and it will be done."

I don't feel like I have amazing faith. It's easy to look at the prophets of the Old Testament who told the sun to stand still, defeated armies with clay pots and trumpets or ox goads, and through God raised people from the dead. Or perhaps we think of David defeating a giant with a sling and a stone, Moses parting the Red Sea, or Esther going before King Xerxes. Paul beaten, Peter crucified upside down, or John imprisoned on an island. *They* trusted, *they* had faith. But do we have that kind of faith? Can we?

The verse above says it doesn't matter how big our faith is. If we simply have faith as small as a mustard seed and do not doubt, Scripture says we can command mountains to throw themselves into the sea. Mountains!

In her article, my friend pointed out that not only can we throw literal mountains into the sea, but we have the power and authority to throw the other mountains in front of us as well—the mental mountains, the emotional mountains, the mountains of sickness, the mountains in relationships. We do not need to be paralyzed by them.

What about when God doesn't move the mountains, though? When He knows it is better that they stay, or that the removal of them is delayed? That is when faith and trust become all the more difficult, and yet all the more important.

When God doesn't move those mountains, will we continue to trust, to obey, to have faith when the physical pain doesn't leave but only increases? When the future that we wanted gets further and further out of reach as our sickness causes us to get further and further behind in school or life? When friends disappear and family members struggle? When God's gifts seem to only get harder, and for once we want just a plain and simple obviously beautiful gift that brings laughter instead of tears?

Now faith is confidence in what we hope for and assurance about what we do not see.
(Hebrews 11:1)

Faith is not just accepting circumstances but trusting that God is working in them for good. Faith means taking the persevering to a new level, letting go, and trusting—truly, trusting—fully and completely.

"How we respond to the unexplained is infinitely more important than getting an explanation for the unexplained." -Dan Hall

Facing the Unknowns

One of the hardest parts of illness is the unknowns. There are so many of them. Not just one mountain, but a whole range of them. And often the mist is so heavy we can't even see what the mountain looks like. How do you find a path over or around it when you can't see your feet? What if you fall off a cliff you didn't even know was there?

Unknowns. Lack of diagnosis. Not many who have gone before you. Questions. What-ifs. What are we to do with them?

The only thing worse than seeing a spider is the one you lose. The things you can't see are the things that are scariest. The human imagination is a powerful thing, and when it concerns chronic illness, it's even more difficult because so many things *are* possible . . . even likely. All you have to do is pick up a pharmaceutical bottle of medication and read the possible side effects. And that's just the side effects of the *medication* that is supposed to *help*.

133

Trust. It all comes down to if we trust that God's plan for us is perfect. If we trust that He is both good and all-powerful. In complete control. Because guess what? What is unknown to us is known to God. The questions we have, God already has answers to. He isn't surprised by the things that have you shocked like a deer in the headlights.

"Never be afraid to trust an unknown future to a known God."
-Corrie ten Boom

So then, what do we do when God decides to keep the answers to Himself? We trust. We trust that He knows what is best and that He will give us the answers we need as we need them . . . in His perfect timing. We have faith that He knows what's best for us and that in His love He will guide us.

A Mountain-Guide

Sometimes when navigating through the valleys and cliffs of the mountains in front of you or surrounding you, it is helpful to have a guide—someone who has walked the path before, who knows the pitfalls and shortcuts.

For anyone, but especially teenagers, it is helpful to open ourselves up to others who have walked through faith in the midst of illness. It is wise for us to accept advice, and even embrace it. As I've said many times before, we were not created to be alone. We don't have to fight this by ourselves. Often, we need help.

Surely you need guidance to wage war, and victory is won through many advisers.
(Proverbs 24:6)

What Does the Future Look Like?

Trusting God with the future may be one of the most difficult parts of faith—trusting Him with the unknown, with the lack of diagnosis, with not understanding what's happening or where this is going.

I've experienced this for myself and still do. I spent nine months with no diagnosis. We spent five or so months with no idea where we would be living the next week or the next day. I've asked the questions: Why? Where? What? Will I ever be able to have a family? Get married? Be a parent? Will I ever be able to live where I want to? What will happen to me? Will this last forever? Will it ever end? Is there something I could have done differently? Can I finish school? Go to college?

Trusting God with the future can be so hard. But . . .

Your eyes saw my unformed body; all the days ordained for me were written in your book before one of them came to be. (Psalm 139:16)

God sees our future, He knows the plans He has for us. He's making diamonds. I've said it before, I'll say it again: He knows what He's doing! We can trust God with our futures because He knows exactly what they hold. He created them. We can trust Him with the unknown, because He is all-powerful and perfect, and because the future is not unknown to Him. He is good. He is perfectly good, and He is our loving Father.

Let's talk more about the all-powerful part. All-powerful means that He can and will give to us all the gifts He wants to, and no one can stop Him. He is a loving Father who doesn't have to worry about money, or human limitations, or how to find the best doctor. He is the Great Physician! And *nothing* can stand in His way or against His plan for our lives.

"Remember this, keep it in mind, take it to heart, you rebels. Remember the former things, those of long ago; I am God, and there is no other; I am God, and there is none like me. I make known the end from the beginning, from ancient times, what is still to come. I say, 'My purpose will stand, and I will do all that I please.' From the east I summon a bird of prey; from a far-off land, a man to fulfill my purpose. What I have said, that I will bring about; what I have planned, that I will do. Listen to me, you stubborn-hearted, you who are now far from my righteousness. I am bringing my righteousness

near, it is not far away; and my salvation will not be delayed. I will grant salvation to Zion, my splendor to Israel. (Isaiah 46:8–13)

When Dreams Die

When you are sick for long periods of time—be it months or years—often dreams either die or seem like they have to die. Maybe you miss out on things you really want, or things that everyone else is doing. Maybe it's learning to drive, or even as simple as going to a birthday party. Or maybe it's bigger things, like your dream job or going to college. These things just can't happen sometimes when you are sick with a long-term illness.

What if you never get better? Do you have to really give up on these dreams of yours? Are they really completely lost to you? It sure feels like it, right? And . . . sometimes they are. In those cases, I think of this quote:

"There are far, far better things ahead than any we leave behind." *-C.S. Lewis*

I know this doesn't sound like much comfort now, but it's true. God says to delight in Him and He will give us the desires of our heart (see Psalm 37:4), and that as our Father, He certainly knows how to give good gifts to us. He loves to bless us, and He loves to make us happy. But first, we may have to learn joy. And He knows what makes us happy better than we do.

However, the story doesn't always end there. As Laura Story explains in her book *When God Doesn't Fix It,* God can resurrect dreams even when they seem to have died, and even after we've attempted to bury them. Just like Jesus resurrected Lazarus for His glory, He can resurrect our dreams if He chooses—they just have to die first.

Mary and Martha recognized this. Even though they were devastated at their brother's death, they still trusted that Jesus had everything under control. I'm sure they wished that Lazarus hadn't died—

desperately! But God resurrected him. As soon as they surrendered Lazarus to God, He gave their brother back to them.

I know this is hard to hear now, and it doesn't necessarily make things easier. I know. But don't let go of this truth, don't let go of hope. Yes, surrender it to God, but don't bury it so deep that you're not willing to let the dream be resurrected by God if He chooses to.

Maybe it feels so far beyond reach it seems impossible . . . but what's impossible with man is possible with God. How dare we doubt His power!

Just look at what I wrote July 2017:

I dream of being a wife and a mother someday. I dream of being a writer and an author. I dream of being a missionary. But how can I be a wife and a helper when I need so much help myself? How can I parent children someday if I can't even manage myself? How can I be a writer if I can't even answer my mom's simple question? How can I be a missionary if I can't leave the house? For so many very big reasons, it feels like those can't happen in the ways that I dream of. It's hard because these are good dreams, they feel like God-given dreams, even! But guys, God knows what He is doing. He does. He even has the power to resurrect those dreams even if we never get better!

So I choose to surrender my dreams to Him, to let them die if they have to. But I will also choose to still hope and pray that God may resurrect them if it is in His will. I choose to trust that He knows what is best for me. I choose to ask God to help me to let go of my grasp on these dreams and choose to leave it all in His hands. It isn't easy, and I know this. But my dreams are not mine to fulfill. I choose to pray for God's dreams.

A friend recently pointed out something I had noticed as well: God is already taking some of my dead or dying dreams and is resurrecting them. Cough-cough. For example, the dream of being a writer and an author. Just look at what you have in your hands right now. So don't lose hope.

Moses' passion was to help his people. But he had one problem. He had just killed an Egyptian. Oops? Found out, he fled to the desert. His dream and passion for his people appeared to be squashed. Discarded. Finished. He was forty years old and a murderer. His own people scoffed at him. Some help he was.

But as we know, that was only the beginning. God took him into the desert and for the next forty years, He prepared and shaped Moses. Wouldn't you have given up and quit after forty years? Wouldn't you question why God would lead you to the desert to spend forty years while your people suffered and died under oppression? I know I probably would.

But here's the thing: God will wait until we're ready. He knows what He's doing. He is patient. He allows us to prepare and get equipped. In fact, He trains us Himself, even when we don't know how to go about it. Often, like Mr. Miyagi, He trains us without us even knowing it.

He will privately train and tutor us until we are ready. He won't send us to defeat an army until we know how to use a sword.

Moses *thought* he was ready . . . but he was forty years too early. God took the fiery man who would kill a random Egyptian and turned him into what the Bible calls "the most humble man in all the world" (see Numbers 12:3). It took him forty years to learn to let go of his plans and his pride until his full confidence was in God, not himself.

And then... God allowed him to be instrumental in freeing Israel and leading them to the promised land and through the desert. After God used forty years to soften and train Moses, He had Moses lead the Israelites through the desert for forty years themselves as they were made into diamonds. God transformed a rebellious nation into one that would trust Him when He told them to walk around a city for seven days without speaking as the inhabitants of Jericho hurled insults at them. God not only resurrected Moses' dream but expanded it beyond imagining in ways Moses could never understand.

Trust God's Plans

It hurts when dreams die and plans change. Sickness isn't fun or desirable no matter how beautiful or strong the diamond is that God is making us into through it. Sometimes—a lot of times—I just want everything to go back to how it was. I don't care about all the wonderful gifts God has given me through my illness, I just want the Sara I used to be back. Have you ever felt that way? I would hazard a guess you have.

Just a few days ago, I laid my head in my dad's lap and cried. "I just want to be a normal person," I told him. I didn't care that I could clearly see how God was using that particular thing to teach me a valuable lesson. I didn't want to learn the lesson. I just wanted to feel fine. To feel like a normal person, even though I knew I didn't actually want to be a "typical teenager."

Maybe God's plans for my future were amazing, but like Esau when he sold his birthright for a bowl of stew, I felt willing to trade my future for momentary relief from discomfort. I wanted my small, old dreams back. I didn't want the amazing new things I knew God had in store. As I could have guessed, the Bible has something to say about that. Let's look at 1 Samuel 16:1. Saul has been rejected by God as king, and God is about to send the prophet Samuel to anoint David to be the new king. Look at what it says:

The Lord said to Samuel, "How long will you mourn for Saul, since I have rejected him as king over Israel? Fill your horn with oil and be on your way; I am sending you to Jesse of Bethlehem. I have chosen one of his sons to be king."

How long will we mourn? Are we mourning the Sauls in our lives when we could be rejoicing over the Davids? I know I have been guilty of it. But ask anyone, and clearly, David was a better king for Israel. So, let's trust God's plans. Let's stop mourning for the Saul that is getting in the way of embracing whatever the David is that God is bringing into our lives through illness. It's okay to mourn the things illness has stolen. It's crucial, even. But we shouldn't let it prevent us from stepping forward into the plans God has for us.

Trusting God's Future Gifts

I've learned to see my sickness as a gift. Over time, God has opened my eyes to see His many blessings in the midst of sickness, to trust His perfect plans in the trials. I learned to think of my trials as a beautiful gift and blessing. Hard, yes. Not necessarily what I would have chosen, but a blessing because it's what God chose for me.

A gift.

However, this has recently posed a problem I wasn't expecting. As God fulfills more and more of those dreams that I had let die, as He resurrects them, I'm hesitant to embrace them.

What? Why?

Well, as God begins to present me with new gifts, I find myself facing the fear that they might be like the last gift God gave me. Of course, I know that He knows best, but I find myself afraid of receiving another "hard" gift. A "gift in disguise." Do you know what I mean?

The gifts God has been giving me, the dreams He's resurrected . . . it isn't even logical to be afraid that they might be the kind wrapped in ugly paper, beautiful underneath. The ones I find myself hesitant to embrace already seem to be wrapped in beautiful paper on the outside to match the beautiful gift on the inside. But I wasn't sure if I could trust the gifts. I was afraid to get my hopes up in case this gift turned back to bite.

Yes, I still saw it as a gift, but I wasn't having faith. I was trusting, but my trust was guarded . . . it was a mental trust and not a whole-heart trust.

The truth that I needed to remember, learn, and hold onto was this: God's goodness. God's perfect goodness. The Bible tells us over and over again of God's unceasing and unimaginable love. It says that He *is* love. We see that He works out everything for the good of those who love Him (see Romans 8:28). We see that He wants to give us blessings and good things. We are told to taste and see that the Lord is good, blessed is the one who takes refuge in Him (see Psalm 34:8). He does not waste a single one of our tears, and He does not desire His precious children to face pain or suffering. We brought that on ourselves because of sin.

If you, then, though you are evil, know how to give good gifts to your children, how much more will your Father in heaven give good gifts to those who ask him! (Matthew 7:11)

We are God's beloved, His cherished, His chosen! He is our Father, our good and perfect King! He created gifts in the first place. God is good. Will we trust that? Believe that? Will we choose to stand on God's promises, knowing that they are yeses and amens? Has God ever failed us? If He has held our lives perfectly in our past, already proving that His plans are to prosper and not to harm—that they are good and perfect—will we not stand on the promises that He has proclaimed concerning our future?

That's the kind of faith that can stare down mountains.

Take It Deeper

- In this chapter, we talked about faith in the unknowns, in the face of mountains, and in the face of dying dreams or plans for the future.
- Pray the following (feel free to change it to your own words): *"God, I give up all my dreams—even good, God-honoring dreams—to You. They are not mine to make happen or to fulfill. I surrender them to You and ask that You will replace them with Your dreams for me. Your plans for my life. I surrender them to You, trusting and knowing that as I let them die, as I let go of my hold on them, You can resurrect them in Your time. Maybe it won't be until Heaven, but I*

leave that in Your hands, my King. These things cannot happen in my own power. I surrender my dreams that seem to have died with this sickness, that I'm struggling to see the possibility in . . .

- o

- o

- o

- *Please help me let go."*

- Do you stand on the promises of God in your life? Especially for your future? I know that this is a lesson God still continues to teach me: how to stand with confidence on His promises. If you struggle with this (or even if you don't), take a moment to look up the following Scriptures containing God's promises for your life. Read them, speak them, pray through them, and choose to stand on God's promises.

  - o Jeremiah 29:11

  - o Revelation 21:4

  - o Isaiah 55:12

  - o 1 Corinthians 2:9/Isaiah 64:4

  - o Ephesians 1

12. In My Weakness

"Lord, is it possible that even in this You can be glorified?! You keep telling me that You love me. All I find when I come to You is mercy, love, and grace. Oh, Jesus how can it be? I'm truly not a disgrace? Oh, Lord how wonderful You are."
-Sara's journal, December 29, 2016

Moses is before God in the wilderness. He has seen the burning bush, and God has given him his calling: "Go tell Pharaoh, the ruler of Egypt, to set My people free!" But while Moses has seen his people's suffering up close and personal, he is unsure. *Me? You really want me? Are You sure, God? What if they don't listen to me?*

So, God gives him amazing signs to perform. God tells Moses to throw his staff down. Moses does so. It becomes a snake! Moses runs. Literally, the Bible tells us that Moses runs from the tools God is giving him.

My brother went through a phase where he was very into snakes. He would research them and learn to identify them. He even found a few four-inch ones to keep as pets. As it turns out, in Florida, there are a lot of snakes. Once, we found a diamondback rattlesnake in our pool filter. (Thankfully, my sister got out of the water in time.) Another time, my mom ran from a snake, leaving shoes behind at the beach . . . you'd have to ask my siblings, as I still haven't been able to sort out all the details of what happened. I wasn't there, you see.

Yet another time, we found a good-sized black racer in a bush by our house. My brother was determined to catch it. He thrust his hands into the bush, trying to grab right behind its head. He ended up grabbing the middle of the snake instead. It thrashed and squirmed and bit, and he continued trying to find and pin down the head. All said and done, he had nine good snakebites by the time it was safely in a container. We admired it and took pictures, and eventually walked it down to a nearby retention pond and released it. Snakes are fast swimmers. Although, I suppose black racers are just fast in general. The point is this: you don't want to just randomly pick up snakes without knowing what you are bargaining for. And from the way Moses ran, I would guess that picking up snakes wasn't part of his daily routine. And yet, still, Moses chooses to obey when God tells him to reach out and *pick up the snake*. Talk about faith.

When Moses obeys God, the snake turns back into a staff. In addition, God gives Moses the second sign of healing: turning a healthy hand into a leprous one and back again.

Then the Lord said, "If they do not believe you or pay attention to the first sign, they may believe the second. But if they do not believe these two signs or listen to you, take some water from the Nile and pour it on the dry ground. The water you take from the river will become blood on the ground." (Exodus 4:8–9)

But Moses isn't convinced. Yes, he believes in God's power. But he doubts his own ability. Mary, the mother of Jesus, was the same way. When Gabriel told her that she would bear the Messiah, she wasn't sure. *"Me? Really? But . . . I'm a virgin!"* Not to mention Gideon. But with God all things are possible. Read the next part of Moses' story carefully, and see if you can relate:

Moses said to the Lord, "Pardon your servant, Lord. I have never been eloquent, neither in the past nor since you have spoken to your servant. I am slow of speech and tongue."

The Lord said to him, "Who gave human beings their mouths? Who makes them deaf or mute? Who gives them sight or makes them blind? Is it not I, the Lord? Now go; I will help you speak and will teach you what to say."

But Moses said, "Pardon your servant, Lord. Please send someone else."

Then the Lord's anger burned against Moses and he said, "What about your brother, Aaron the Levite? I know he can speak well. He is already on his way to meet you, and he will be glad to see you. You shall speak to him and put words in his mouth; I will help both of you speak and will teach you what to do. He will speak to the people for you, and it will be as if he were your mouth and as if you were God to him. But take this staff in your hand so you can perform the signs with it." (Exodus 4:10–17)

Like Moses, I struggle with my weakness. Pardon me, Lord. Pardon Your servant, but are You sure? Are You certain I'm the right person? I'm young, I'm weak, I'm inexperienced, I'm sick, I'm sinful, I'm not qualified, I'm not enough, I'm not eloquent, I'm not the right person. Moses stutters, but I fill-in-the-blank! We don't understand how God's plan is going to work out, we don't see how He can possibly accomplish in us the things we feel Him calling us to. Especially in sickness.

I share this because it is a huge personal struggle for me. Over and over, even though I have seen God's power and His working in the past, I wonder if I'm really able to do what He is asking of me. I want to . . . I've seen the need and the suffering, but am I qualified to take action?

The thing is, that doesn't matter.

At all.

Because it's not me. God doesn't ask me to do it in my own strength, and woe be to me if I tried! The Bible says that He uses the weak things of this world—the things that are not—to shame the wise. It says that the foolishness of God is wiser than human wisdom, and the weakness of God is stronger than human strength for His glory (see 1 Corinthians 1:25, 27–28).

As God equipped Moses with miracles, He will equip us to accomplish what He has asked of us. We can ask questions . . . Moses clearly did. And God provided Aaron in response to it. But notice how God still says, "But take your staff." God's saying, "Okay, Moses, I will give you Aaron, but trust Me. I know what I'm doing. I already provided you with what you need."

God is already prepared for our weakness. In fact, during Moses' conversation with God, God had already sent Aaron on his way. God knew that Moses would need help, and so He had Aaron start his journey to Moses before Moses even asked. God didn't say, "Aw, Moses, I'm sorry for your speech struggles." Instead, He gave Moses tools and signs that would glorify Himself.

But he said to me, "My grace is sufficient for you, for my power is made perfect in weakness." Therefore I will boast all the more gladly about my weaknesses, so that Christ's power may rest on me. (2 Corinthians 12:9)

His Power Made Perfect

This has been a struggle for me especially in writing this book. As I write it, I wrestle with constant doubts, all the way from chapter one until now as we approach the end of this book. I don't feel qualified. I don't feel like I can live up to the expectations that people (including myself) have of me. After all, I'm just a teenager and have only been sick for just over two years. What do I know? But again, it's not about me. It's about God, whose power is made perfect in our weakness, whose grace is sufficient.

Maybe you are a sick teenager and you feel useless. You feel unworthy and unusable. Let me tell you the truth: that is a lie! God is equipping you for precious things to come, even if you can't see them yet. He is working all things together for the good of those who love Him.

Now may the God of peace, who through the blood of the eternal covenant brought back from the dead our Lord Jesus, that great

Shepherd of the sheep, equip you with everything good for doing his will, and may he work in us what is pleasing to him, through Jesus Christ, to whom be glory forever and ever. Amen.
(Hebrews 13:20–21)

This book isn't the only area in which I've struggled with this, however. For several years before getting sick I participated in various discipleship groups. Some were led by my mom for me and other girls my age, and others I led for my younger sister and other girls.

Due to health-related things, however, we had to take a break from those for a few months. God still put a passion in my heart to disciple younger girls, but for now, it would have to wait.

Well, when the time came—our life was less chaotic—and I was able to start a group again, I was afraid to do it. You'd think it would have been easier this time than starting groups in the past. I mean, this was going to be the third group I would have led, after all. But my problem wasn't normal nerves about getting up and talking in front of a group.

This was different. I was afraid because I no longer trusted myself. I no longer had confidence in myself. In the intervening time, I had become intimately familiar with my own weaknesses, and I wasn't sure I was qualified to be teaching other girls' hearts. Besides that, there were the practical things that came with still being sick. I had brain fog . . . could I even communicate God's truth in a way that made sense? My sickness was unpredictable . . . was I really ready to commit to being there and teaching every two weeks?

As with this book, however, it didn't matter. My own power, my own strength, and my own eloquence wasn't the question. The question was if I would rely on God's power, strength, and words. Would I trust that He was powerful enough to work through my failures and weaknesses?

I decided to go ahead with it. There were some bumps in the road, but God worked all the details out, answering my prayers. As He brought everything together, orchestrating it all, it became amazingly clear that it wasn't me at all who was responsible for the group's success. It was God. And because I wasn't capable in my own power, God's glory was more clearly shown.

I have seen this same truth over and over again in my life. In fact, I think that learning my own weakness is one of the most valuable lessons I've learned through my sickness. First, because it teaches me humility, and second because it allows God to work more clearly and powerfully in my life! In our weakness, God's power is made *perfect.*

Boasting about Your Weakness

People who are chronically ill often have a hard time talking about their sickness. And for good reason—we don't want people to mock or disbelieve us; we don't want to complain; we don't want people to get freaked out; and we don't think they will understand. It's easier to pretend to be healthy. It's easier to hide our pain. It's also just plain difficult to talk about. There are memories that hurt to relive, and we don't want to share our deepest struggles with the world. Our pride also sometimes gets in the way.

Yet in 2 Corinthians 12:9 Paul speaks about boasting in his weakness. Why? So that Christ's power may rest on him. So that God may be glorified even more.

"When I prayed for transparency, I didn't picture this!"
-Sara's journal, October 2016

In your sickness, God has given you an incredible story. He has thrown something *huge* at you. And it is your choice how you will respond to it. You can fight the dark, painful struggle and have the testimony of overcoming it, of facing it with growing trust, faith, and joy. Or you can get lost in the despair that is always lurking, fighting to overwhelm your defenses. You can get lost in pain, self-pity, suffering, and sickness.

Make your decision well, for it has such great potential and power to change the lives of those around you, even if you never talk to them (or them to you). I never realized how many people were watching as I spent months in my lonely, quiet bedroom, or when my family spent weeks driving here and there searching for a place to live, or when we threw away everything we owned. But they were.

When I prayed for transparency, I was thinking that people would be able to see God working in my struggles with sin, or with whatever. However, I didn't picture that they would be seeing me when my brain was loopy and I couldn't follow more than three words at a time. I didn't think that the transparency would mean the slightest chemical made me break down in tears—no matter where I was or who I was with. I didn't imagine that transparency would be my exhaustion and pain that was a walk to the mailbox.

Those around me saw me completely fallen apart. I pictured that people seeing my transparency would be them seeing how God brought me through some dark trial or struggle and how He allowed me to amazingly overcome it. But instead, they saw my worst—my mind turned to a child's, where my best description was "Umm, I feel like . . . fuzz."

Definitely not the admiration I was unconsciously imagining. I tried hiding for a while. Since I couldn't trust my mind to make logical sentences, I hid behind not saying as much. I was afraid I would say something wrong, or hurt someone, or simply embarrass myself. And trust me, that isn't me! Plus, I couldn't hide it. And you know what? I shouldn't. Didn't I ask God to teach me transparency?

I'm not saying that you have to share your deepest darkest struggles with the world. That isn't healthy or appropriate. And I know that it's different for everyone. For me personally, I know that God has called me to boast in my weakness for His glory. Even though there are times when I don't want to share my story, He has allowed me to see Him using it to encourage other people over and over again. The struggle you are facing and how God has helped you through it may be exactly what someone else needs to hear . . . just do it with God's discernment.

Our story is not our own . . . *God* is the author, He wrote it and it belongs to Him. Should it not bring Him glory?

Your eyes saw my unformed body; all the days ordained for me were written in your book before one of them came to be.
(Psalm 139:16)

If you're like me, it is simply impossible to tell your story and not tell of God.

One final note, though: transparency is *not* the same as drama. Drama comes from a selfish desire for attention and gossip. Which, sadly, teenagers are known for. Drama often includes complaining, and really is just all about us. The way to identify the difference between drama and transparency is by our motive. Is our goal to encourage others by sharing what God is doing in our lives or to ask for accountability or prayer? That's healthy and needed. But is it to complain, talk about ourselves, and get others to agree with our list of suffering? That's drama . . . which is best to avoid. One is about us, the other is about bringing glory to God and doing our best to please Him.

Serving God When You're Sick

Okay, let's summarize this chapter real fast:

1. God isn't surprised by our weakness.

2. Our weakness is for God's glory.

3. God uses our weakness.

4. God's grace is sufficient in our weakness.

5. We should share our story and be open about our weakness.

Sound right? Good. The thing about God's grace being sufficient in our weakness isn't that we are just able to relax about the things we can't do. It isn't just that God will close the gap and pick up the slack. It's that God will still work through us in our weakness by His power in us. Hear that? God's unmatchable power at work *in us*.

We can still serve God even though we are sick. We can have mercy on ourselves, of course. We need to. But here I want to share a few ways that we can serve God by His grace, even while sick. Yes, each of our capabilities are different. However, there *are* ways you can serve God from bed, or stuck at home. The great thing about serving God is that it isn't one size fits all. There isn't a formula you have to follow or else you aren't serving Him. We can be creative.

For example, maybe we can't be hospitable in a typical way, but we can be hospitable by being open to talking with people or listening to them . . . even via online communication or text if we can't handle a phone conversation. Being hospitable to people's hearts is more important than having a neatly kept house for people to briefly admire or freshly baked brownies to temporarily fill their stomachs. It is better to minister to the soul than the body. After all, the soul is what lasts forever. Of course, as you know, practical hospitality and care are important too, but it's okay if we are too sick to do so (for whatever reason).

We may not be able to be a missionary, but we can pray. We can fight the spiritual battles behind the scenes while others fight them in the normal ways. Just go back to chapter ten to see how powerful prayer is!

Perhaps we can't physically go walk around and evangelize, but we can have courage in talking about Jesus to our doctors, nurses, and others we come in contact with.

Maybe we aren't able to serve at a soup kitchen, but we can do our best to make things easy for our caregivers and family members.

Think about your unique abilities . . . and disabilities. How can they be used to glorify God? For example, I love to write. I may not be able to do anything else, but something I can do (some of the time) is write from my bed. So I do.

I'm not physically able to do the activities that would build friendships with other people where I live. I don't know very many people here in Arizona. But I am able to be online, and God has enabled me to get to know many people all over the world and to be a friend to them that way.

Be creative! Just because you are sick doesn't mean you can't serve God. Just hanging in there and persevering is serving God. Your silent suffering is seen by others more than you realize.

For just as each of us has one body with many members, and these members do not all have the same function, so in Christ we, though many, form one body, and each member belongs to all the others. (Romans 12:4–5)

Grace for Ourselves

"Okay, okay," you say, "I get it. God's grace is sufficient for me. He isn't upset by the things I can't do or surprised by my weakness. He is actually glorified." But there is something crucial we still need to discuss.

You guessed it (I blame the title of this section): having grace for ourselves. Sometimes, it can be so much easier to have grace for others than it is to have grace for ourselves. Maybe God can have grace for you, but you of all people know just how much you do not deserve grace. So even though God has given us grace, we continue to try and push ourselves and punish ourselves. We surround ourselves with guilt that isn't coming from anywhere but ourselves (and definitely not from God).

There are a few problems with that course of action. First, God sees our hearts even more clearly than we do. He knows our sin . . . Jesus paid the price for it: death. Every lash of the whip, every second of agony, He felt. Oh, He knows our sin *way* better than we do. And yet He shows grace.

In fact, if we continue to refuse to give grace to ourselves, we are taking from the whole point of Jesus' sacrifice: grace and forgiveness. Freedom from sin, guilt, and condemnation.

"Come to me, all you who are weary and burdened, and I will give you rest. Take my yoke upon you and learn from me, for I am gentle and humble in heart, and you will find rest for your souls. For my yoke is easy and my burden is light."
(Matthew 11:28–30)

Maybe you aren't sure that you can have grace for yourself. But that's okay. All you have to do is ask God to help you. Ask Him to put *His* grace in your heart. Your best is enough. Rest in that. Choose right now to have grace for your own weaknesses. Make sure that you are only carrying the burden and yoke that God means for you to carry.

We think that we can do it all ourselves and that we are self-sustaining. But we aren't. If we rely on God, though, and live in obedience to Him and not in obedience to what we think we should be doing, He will provide the power, strength, and ability to do what He wants us to do. He doesn't expect us to serve Him by ourselves.

After all, God came down to be with us, rather than expecting us to be able to come up and be with Him. *He* saved us from our sins when He knew we could not do it ourselves. He sees our weaknesses and loves us anyway. He sees our weaknesses and still allows us to serve Him in mighty ways. God is not limited by our weakness.

In fact, this is love for God: to keep his commands. And his commands are not burdensome, for everyone born of God overcomes the world. This is the victory that has overcome the world, even our faith. Who is it that overcomes the world? Only the one who believes that Jesus is the Son of God. (1 John 5:3–5)

Take It Deeper

- Second Corinthians 12:9 has become my favorite Bible verse throughout this illness journey. Every time I talk to someone else with a chronic or long-term illness, this is the verse I want to share with them. So of course, I want to continue that by sharing it with you.

- If you can, I would suggest memorizing it, but if not, then write it down somewhere you will see it every day. Please don't ever forget that God's grace is sufficient for you and that His power is made perfect in your weakness. And don't forget to have grace for yourself.

13. He's Making Diamonds

"Father, make me a lobster. Take my dragon-skin off all the way. Lord, I choose to hide in Your wings while my first shell is ripped off and my slimy, vulnerable squishiness is revealed, until my new shell grows on. I suppose I never want to leave Your shelter. If I do it will be time for growing again. Father, why does it take so much and so long to be made?"
-Sara's journal, May 2016

Diamonds. As we come to the close of this book, I find I should make sure to explain the beautiful picture of diamonds. You may have guessed at it already . . . there have been lots of hints and references to diamonds all throughout this book. But it is such an amazing truth we should keep in mind that I want to devote this final chapter to it.

However, before explaining diamonds, let's talk about lobsters. Yes, lobsters. I promise it relates. You may remember me mentioning some of our adventures in Montana. While we were there, we lived at a soon-to-be missionary school that would train people to help trafficked women. At the time, though, it wasn't quite up and running, and we were working on construction.

In the woods there were about forty that hadn't been lived in or taken care of for years. While we were there, an older man briefly came into our lives for about a week. He was from South America, and I don't know how the conversation started, but he began to share this great analogy . . . about lobsters.

He explained that when lobsters shed their shells, it's a painful process. And a dangerous one. When they remove them, they are left with a slimy, vulnerable squishiness, and they have to take shelter until their new shell grows—which takes a lot out of them.

Sometimes, I feel like a lobster. First, I had the traumatic removal of my shell, and now I have no choice but to take refuge in my Father's wings as the new shell slowly—oh so slowly—grows back on.

Therefore, if anyone is in Christ, the new creation has come: The old has gone, the new is here! (2 Corinthians 5:17)

The diamond analogy is sort of like the lobster one. In our trials, in our sickness, God is making us into diamonds. Through the painful process of removing our lobster shell, He is removing our pride, our self-reliance, and our sin. He is making us stronger, more mature, and more compassionate.

If we let Him.

He is making us into a new creation, making us more and more like Him every day. He isn't wasting our pain or our tears. He is accomplishing His perfect plan and purpose. He is making diamonds out of us.

For he does not willingly bring affliction or grief to anyone. (Lamentations 3:33)

Over and over again, I have seen that He has had a plan in it all and a purpose for the pain, that He truly has been making diamonds out of us. He doesn't have us in this trial for no reason! Through it, He has enabled me to connect with people I never would have otherwise. God has taught me about things I would never have known and brought me to so many places I would never have gone. He has shaped my heart, brought me to my knees, and given me strength I would never have known. I praise Him!

Losing Sight of Diamonds

There are times, however, when that is difficult to see. All we see are the trials, the fire, and the suffering, and we lose sight of what God is making through it. We lose sight of the fact that He has a plan and a purpose. We know that He was with us, but instead of focusing on Him, we just focus on enduring. We get fixated on the fire and become blind to the gold that fire refines. Focused on trouble rather than love. But God already sees the fire. There is no need to be obsessively concerned about it.

Therefore, since we are surrounded by such a great cloud of witnesses, let us throw off everything that hinders and the sin that so easily entangles. And let us run with perseverance the race marked out for us, fixing our eyes on Jesus, the pioneer and perfecter of faith. For the joy set before him he endured the cross, scorning its shame, and sat down at the right hand of the throne of God. Consider him who endured such opposition from sinners, so that you will not grow weary and lose heart.
(Hebrews 12:1–3)

We have to fix our eyes on Jesus, on the goal, the prize! If all we see is the pain and suffering, we won't be able to make it to the finish line, to the joy set before us. We must not forget that God has a purpose in the pain and a plan for us. His plans for us are still to prosper, they are still for good. We cannot forget that. He loves His children and only desires what is best for us. He doesn't delight in our pain, but He knows what He is doing. He will not give us anything beyond what we can bear. Let us not lose sight of diamonds.

Don't Reject the Promised Land Because of the Desert

"I'll lead you to the promised land," God tells the Israelites.

"But we want to go back to Egypt!" they whine.

As my brother said in observation of the Israelites, "Are they dumb?" You'd think it would be a no-brainer. Promised land, with milk and honey and safety? Or Egypt, with slavery and oppression and suffering?

When we read the Bible, it seems like God chose the most rebellious, unfaithful, plain old *difficult* nation to be His special people. Yet . . . I have to confess, I relate to the Israelites more than I'd like to admit. I see myself in them, in their stubbornness, their blindness, and their foolishness.

Reading through the first few books of the Bible, I came to a realization.

My life used to be much simpler. Easier. More normal. Sometimes, I find myself wishing for my Egypt back. Not that my life was difficult before illness like the Israelites' lives before the wilderness, but it sure was easier. And as much as I long for the promised land that God is bringing me to through this illness—the diamonds He is making—I don't want to go through the wilderness to get there. I'd rather teleport from here to there without taking the time to build the muscle and understand the gift (not to mention go through the suffering, of course).

Wilderness is *hard.* Imagine that.

So often we get so caught up in what our life used to be that we seem blind to the diamonds and amazing, wonderful gifts God is giving us in our new season of life!

"Forget the former things; do not dwell on the past. See, I am doing a new thing! Now it springs up; do you not perceive it? I am making a way in the wilderness and streams in the wasteland."
(Isaiah 43:18–19)

The wilderness is worth it to get to the promised land.

And—as always—God has us in the wilderness for a reason. There is a reason that He didn't just teleport the Israelites (or us) straight to the promised land. All you have to do is read the first five books of the Bible to see the change between the Israelites who crossed the Red Sea on dry land only to whine about food and water the next day, to the Israelites who had been refined and trusted God as they humbly and obediently entered the promised land at last.

"Therefore I am now going to allure her; I will lead her into the wilderness and speak tenderly to her. There I will give her back her vineyards, and will make the Valley of Achor a door of hope. There she will respond as in the days of her youth, as in the day she came up out of Egypt." (Hosea 2:14–15)

Nurse Logs

We were hiking with a family friend in the Kettles, an area on Whidbey Island in Washington State.

"See that fallen-down log?" she asked us. My siblings and I craned our necks and spotted what she was pointing to.

"Do you see the saplings growing out of it?" We craned our heads some more.

"That is what is called a nurse log. The old tree has fallen down and died, but the young plants and trees have been able to grow up using the nutrients from the deteriorating tree," she told us.

And years later, I think this picture holds some important truth for those of us being made into diamonds through illness. Maybe like the strong, old tree, things in our lives have had to die because of sickness. Maybe we've been toppled over and broken down by the winds. But God is still using us, perhaps even more so because of our sickness. Through the death of some of our dreams or abilities or plans, He is bringing new life, both in our own lives and into the lives of others.

While we're on the topic of trees, I want to talk a bit about fire. In Florida at one particular state park we frequented, they did controlled burns once or twice a year. Everything would be the usual palmettos and dense underbrush until one day everything was black and charred. Then, a few weeks later, everything would be even greener than before.

Why do foresters do controlled burns? Ironically, to foster new life and fresh growth (as well as prevent worse fires). Controlled burns make the soil more fertile. It clears out underbrush and lets sunlight reach into places it couldn't get to before. It gets rid of the plants that were choking out others and creates room for new plants to grow.

Maybe the plants it gets rid of weren't necessarily bad, but they might have been unintentionally destructive to the plants that needed to grow around them, like plans we might have had for our lives, or obsessions we'd allowed to take over areas of our lives. As we know, sickness forces us to consolidate our priorities and rethink how we use every moment of our lives and every drop of energy.

Fire is part of God's plan both in our lives and in nature. Though God didn't create pain and will eventually take it away (Heaven!), fire is often what we need to grow. Eventually, at the right time, God will send rain, but only once the underbrush that needs to go has been eradicated. As Levi Lusko pointed out in a sermon we listened to, parts of your calling are perhaps heat-activated.

Growing is hard. It takes a lot of fuel and effort. A seedling starts out buried and has to push through the dirt to get to the surface and the sunlight, and then it has to fight off insects and bugs, and search for water . . . but the result is a beautiful flower or a towering, mighty tree. Believe it or not, flowers can grow in the desert. I've seen them bloom on cacti!

He's Making Butterflies

What God is shaping us into—the life He has given us—may not be what we had hoped for. But His plan is even better than our hopes. His dreams are above our dreams. It may not be what we expected or desired, but it is better.

"For my thoughts are not your thoughts, neither are your ways my ways," declares the Lord. "As the heavens are higher than the earth, so are my ways higher than your ways and my thoughts than your thoughts. As the rain and the snow come down from heaven, and do not return to it without watering the earth and making it bud and flourish, so that it yields seed for the sower and bread for the eater . . ." (Isaiah 55:8–10)

For my sixteenth birthday, my mom got me a necklace. Inside the glass is a butterfly wing. (Don't worry, I'm assured that no butterflies were harmed by humans in the making of it.) She explained that though it has been a hard two years—nothing like what I'd imagined my prime teenage years to look like—God was shaping me through them. He had taken me as a small, squishy caterpillar, striped yellow, white, and black, full of leaves—and wrapped me in a cocoon.

In the dark, in the lonely days spent in hiding, spent in bed, He taught me more about who He is and who I am in Him. When I finally thought I had learned the lessons I was supposed to learn, when it seemed He had planned for me to emerge into the light again, I discovered the cocoon. Emerging into the light was difficult . . . my trials were not over yet.

When my siblings and I were younger, we used to catch monarch caterpillars and take care of them. We would feed them milkweed leaves and watch as they grew, growing fat and long until they finally climbed to the top of their cage and made a cocoon.

Let me fill you in on a secret: right before monarch caterpillars hatch from their cocoons, the cocoons turn black. They start out green and eventually start to get a little dark until finally they turn as black as possible. And as soon as they get super dark, you know it is time for the caterpillars to emerge as butterflies.

However, we had been warned. We were not to help them out of their cocoon . . . they had to do it on their own. Otherwise, they would not gain the strength they needed to function and fly later. So,

161

we would watch. The butterflies would emerge from their cocoons looking half-dead. Their wings would be shriveled, and they wouldn't be moving much.

But as they hung on the top of the cage upside-down, having made it through their trial, emerging when their cocoons were blackest, their wings would stretch out to their full width, drying into beautiful orange and black colors. Carefully, we would stick our fingers into the cage, allow the butterflies to climb onto a finger, and transport them outdoors.

Leaving them on a plant, we would watch as they learned to fly. Lifting off and fluttering only to land again a few feet away. With each flight, they would go a little bit farther until finally they were too far away to see.

It was amazing to watch. At the time, I didn't grasp how relatable they were. But for those who are chronically ill, they are. Cocoons, wings, flying . . . those are some scary things. We don't understand what's going on. We don't understand why it is so difficult to grow back our lobster shell or to break through our cocoon. Yet when things are the darkest, God is still there. He has a perfect plan, and He is allowing us to struggle because He knows it will make us stronger. He is making butterflies. Lobsters. Diamonds.

Choose what you will. But do not forget that God has a purpose in your pain. He is refining you as gold and silver, removing the impurities.

This third I will put into the fire; I will refine them like silver and test them like gold. They will call on my name and I will answer them; I will say, 'They are my people,' and they will say, 'The Lord is our God. -Zechariah 13:9

He's shaping us into His image. When the pressure is unbearable, He is making diamonds. When the trials hurt, He is shaping and cutting the diamond into something more beautiful than we can imagine.

Diamonds.

Flowers.

Butterflies.

Gold.

All of them have to go through a difficult refining or growing process to get to the final, beautiful masterpiece they were meant to be. In the words of Treebeard, "Don't be hasty." Growing takes time. As does diamond-making.

And this shaping, this polishing . . . guess what? Though your specific trial may end (and do not lose hope that it will!), the shaping won't. Sanctification, holiness, becoming more Christ-like—that isn't something that ends. It is something that God will be doing every single day of our lives.

If we allow Him.

We will either be growing more and more like Him or further and further from Him. It is our choice. Diamonds are never done . . . even once diamonds are cut and set in a ring, they have to be cleaned, guarded, and cared for. God is constantly growing us. There have been times when I thought I'd learned my lesson. When I asked God why I had to flare again because I was sure I'd already learned everything I needed from a particular type of sickness. Boy, was I wrong. I'll always have more to learn—even from illness. Will we choose to allow Him to shape us into diamonds?

Take It Deeper

- We've come to the end of this book, but likely not the end of your trials or mine. Here is my final challenge to you: Don't stop searching out God's truths in the Bible, don't stop bringing your heart and the hard questions to God. Continue to pursue Him and remember His truths about you, suffering, and Himself.

S.G. Willoughby

Acknowledgments

I never used to read the acknowledgment section in books. But then I became a writer. Now I always do. Just like we need people to come alongside us during trials, books take a team of people as well. This book definitely wasn't produced alone, and I figure this isn't the place to spare words. If this book is a diamond, it's because so many gracious people spent time cutting, refining, and polishing it.

First, to those who read this book even before it was even completed: my amazing Alpha readers. They weathered my moments of both panic and happy dancing, and together they helped me beat my words into submission.

Beckie, my paragraph size perfecter, and who was always one of the first to read each chapter as I sent it. Meagan, my wonderful cheerleader. Courtney, who rescued me from chapter two. Hailey, who said "I relate!" over and over again. Nina, who insisted that I send her chapter one before anyone else got to read it. You are a loyal sister. Ainsley, one of my oldest friends. If it weren't for *Th!nk*, I wouldn't have started my writing journey those years ago. Jessica, who sent me such helpful emails, inspiring me to add sections to each chapter. Natalie, my "sis" who always knew what to say. Emma, who has quietly encouraged me by example as she fights her own battles. Esther, who laughed at Beckie's and my Brian Reagan and *Princess Bride* banter, and who cried with me as I relived memories that were hard to handle.

Each of you did all that and so much more. This book would not be the same without you.

Then we have my awesome beta readers. They read the entire book in two weeks—last minute—to help me meet my deadline. I can't thank them enough.

Angela, who read the book in less than twenty-four hours. Jessica, the wonderful "Just Police." Gabriella, Bethany, Krystle, Adaline, Bekah, and Ella who said "Me, too!" Hannah, who waited so patiently. Christopher and Callie, two of my teammates from *Found Who I Am.* Courtney, who checked every Bible reference in the entire book. Esther, Beckie, and Nina who did more than I have words for. Mama and Daddy whose opinions mean the world to me... you two sincerely liking it meant so much.

Next, we have my awesome editor, Kelsey Bryant. You edited the book even faster than I could hope for and were so gracious.

Thank you also to Kellyn Roth who did a wonderful job formatting my book in such a short time crunch.

Thank you to my brother Silas for helping me record and edit my audiobook (yes, you can be a rapper, Nina), not to mention made a wonderful book trailer. You're pretty cool. Sorry I can be difficult to work with, and thank you for your patience. You did an amazing job.

Thank you to Mama, who taught me to read and write, who didn't teach me grammar, or who taught me how to make wise decisions (apparently books take a lot of those).

Thank you to Jon Steingard for being excited to write a foreword, and for reading the book and sending me the foreword in record time. It was an answer to many prayers.

Thank you to Dan Sirak for the amazing cover! I didn't know exactly what I wanted, but your creation is perfect. It's even better than I could have imagined.

Thank you to my awesome readers . . . Both of my blog and to you who have read this book.

Lastly, thank you to the instructors and students of Young Writer's Workshop. I'd be very lost without your word sprints, wise advice, and discussions.

S.G. Willoughby

References

Chambers, Oswald. *My Utmost for His Highest: The Classic Daily Devotional*. Uhrichsville, OH: Barbour Books, 2015.

Davis, Katie, and Beth Clark. *Kisses from Katie: A Story of Relentless Love and Redemption*. New York: Howard Books, 2011.

Goff, Bob. *Love Does*. Nashville, TN: Thomas Nelson, 2014.

Lewis, C. S., and Clyde S. Kilby. *Letters to an American Lady*. Grand Rapids, MI: William B. Eerdmans Publishing Company, 2014.

Lucado, Max. *Before Amen: The Power of a Simple Prayer*. Thomas Nelson, 2016.

Piper, John. *When I Don't Desire God: How to Fight for Joy*. Crossway Books, 2004.

Smith, Esther. *When Chronic Pain & Illness Take Everything Away: How to Mourn Our Losses*. CreateSpace Independent Publishing Platform, 2016.

Story, Laura, and Jennifer Schuchmann. *When God Doesn't Fix It: Lessons You Never Wanted to Learn, Truths You Can't Live Without*. Thomas Nelson, 2015.

Tolkien, John Ronald Reuel. *The Lord of the Ring* ..London: G. Allen and Unwin, 1970.

Veggie Tales. Produced by Phil Vischer. Performed by Phil Vischer and Mike Nawrocki and Tim Hodge and Lisa Vischer,. Big Idea Entertainment.

Author's Note:
I have tried to source all of the things mentioned, referenced, or quoted in this book to the best of my ability, however, if I have missed anything or you have found more information I was unable to, please contact me via my website sgwilloughby.com so that I can correct it.

94407175R00103

Made in the USA
Lexington, KY
28 July 2018